I0211593

Caring for Students Who Need It Most in
Open Distance E-Learning Environments

Caring for Students Who Need It Most in
Open Distance E-Learning Environments

This Is (Not) Hidden Philosophy

DONIWEN PIETERSEN

foreword by Moeketsi Letseka

RESOURCE *Publications* · Eugene, Oregon

CARING FOR STUDENTS WHO NEED IT MOST IN OPEN
DISTANCE E-LEARNING ENVIRONMENTS
This Is (Not) Hidden Philosophy

Copyright © 2025 Doniwen Pietersen. All rights reserved. Except for brief
quotations in critical publications or reviews, no part of this book may
be reproduced in any manner without prior written permission from the
publisher. Write: Permissions, Wipf and Stock Publishers, 199 W. 8th Ave.,
Suite 3, Eugene, OR 97401.

Resource Publications
An Imprint of Wipf and Stock Publishers
199 W. 8th Ave., Suite 3
Eugene, OR 97401

www.wipfandstock.com

PAPERBACK ISBN: 979-8-3852-5163-6
HARDCOVER ISBN: 979-8-3852-5164-3
EBOOK ISBN: 979-8-3852-5165-0
VERSION NUMBER 08/27/25

To the students of my past, who taught me what it means to care.
To the students of my present, who challenge me to care deeper.
And to the students of my future, who will remind me why caring must never cease—this book is for you.

Contents

List of Figures

Foreword

*Caring for Students Who Need It Most in Open Distance
E-Learning Environments: This is (Not) Hidden Philosophy*

I AM DEEPLY HONORED and humbled to contribute the foreword
to this short, but brilliantly written book, *Caring for Students Who
Need It Most in Open Distance E-Learning Environments: This Is
(Not) Hidden Philosophy*, by Professor Doniwen Pietersen. The
book reflects on the culture of care and inclusion in the context of
open and distance e-learning (ODeL). Prof Pietersen epitomizes
the notion of care and inclusion in the book's declaration:

*"To the students of my past, who taught me what it means to
care. To the students of my present, who challenge me to care deeper.
And to the students of my future, who will remind me why caring
must never cease—this book is for you."*

Prof Pietersen's declaration above resonates with Scottish
moral philosopher Alasdair MacIntyre's ompelling argument in
his book, *After Virtue: A Study in Moral Theory*, that "A proxy entrusted to care for others who are unable to speak should know
and be rooted in relationships with those for whom he or she is
entrusted to speak". In the specific African context, the philosophy
of *Ubuntu* is a particular ethic of care that promotes empathy and
relational autonomy. In line with this book comes an adage with a
similar line of argument and concept based in African philosophy,
"*Botho* or *ubuntu*", which is to be treated as normative in that it
encapsulates moral norms and virtues such as kindness, generos-
ity, compassion, benevolence, courtesy, and respect and concern
for others.

Prof Pietersen teaches philosophy of education in the College of Education (CEDU), at the University of South Africa (UNISA). With students' enrolment estimated to be around 400 000 UNISA is described as a *mega university*. *Caring for Students Who Need It Most in Open Distance E-Learning Environments* is concerned about ways in which lecturers support and nurture students who require the greatest help in ODeL settings. ODeL settings are ideally designed to offer flexibility in teaching and learning by reaching students wherever they are - in their homes, in offices, on holidays, etc. ODeL provides teaching and learning opportunities and resources that enable students to earn higher education qualifications without the requirement to attend traditional in-person classes. It creates opportunities for lifelong learning by removing barriers to access learning; by being student-centered, by providing student support, and by constructing learning programs with the expectation that students can succeed. In ODeL contexts, teaching and learning are leveraged using modern digital technologies such as internet connectivity, reliable Wi-Fi, and the provision of tools of trade, such as laptops, desktops, Tablets, and smartphones. The assumption is that the rapid growth of digital technologies in the advent of the Fourth Industrial Revolution (4IR) and artificial intelligence (AI) in education will be ubiquitous. However, this is debatable in the world where socio-economic inequalities by earnings and geographical locations are rampant. Professor Pietersen is acutely aware of this conundrum: "Addressing the requirements of students who may encounter obstacles because of their socio-economic background, level of digital literacy or emotional health is difficult and calls for a thorough grasp of how to offer fair support in increasingly ODeL and digital environments".

Prof Pietersen mulls over the pervasive socio-economic inequality in South Africa's higher education and the role of caring lecturers. His position is that lecturers must cultivate an environment that recognizes and addresses the diverse needs of students by designing inclusive curricula, employing pedagogical strategies that promote engagement, and providing adequate support tailored to students' varying socioeconomic circumstances (p.2). He argues that "It is the duty of lecturers to democratically involve students in the online teaching and learning process. This is the ultimate goal of all levels of schooling". While "philosophical perspectives on care emphasize the moral responsibility of educators to create inclusive and supportive learning environments" (p.14), "not all instructors take a forward-thinking stance when it comes to their online teaching and learning assignments" (p.9). Education should be shaped by our understanding of the democratic principles, however porous, nebulous, complex, and contested these might be. In this regard, Prof Pietersen draws on Brazilian philosopher of Education, Paulo Freire's landmark book, *Pedagogy of the Oppressed* to argue that "in open distance e-Learning (ODeL) environments, philosophical and dialogical pedagogies rooted in deliberative democracy play a crucial role in fostering an inclusive and caring educational atmosphere". For him, deliberative democracy emphasizes the importance of dialogue and collective reasoning. Educators should therefore cultivate a sense of belonging and agency, particularly for the marginalized sections of society, by creating spaces where students can voice their concerns and contribute meaningfully to discussions.

Prof Pietersen pursues the case for 'dialogue in ODeL' further in Chapter 3: Dialogue and Care for Students in ODeL Environments, in which he "aims to optimize quality education of dialogue and care where skills, values, and equal distribution of resources can be accessed by all". His focus is on ways "to administer clear dialogical and caring aims in online higher education spaces where students can grow holistically and critically...based on how Freire's dialogical theory regarding online higher education can be transformed to facilitate student success and create engagement in student-lecturer relations". In Chapter 4 Prof Pietersen is intentional and assertive that "Teaching and learning in an ODeL environment needs to be based on caring for students who need it most". His assertion is premised on the assumption that "the goal of caring education...is to create well-read, considerate, scholarly people with a strong ability for autonomous critical thought in order to support and contribute to the development of a just and civilized society". An important pearl of wisdom that emerges from Chapter 4 is that "ODeL systems should cultivate an environment of critical, reflective, and compassionate engagement between students and instructors, grounded in an ethic of care".

Chapter 5 examines "how social and cultural capital relate to the provision of care for students in the ODeL setting and assess how deliberative democracy as a feature of online higher education might foster care through discourse". Chapter 6 unpacks South Africa's education system which continues to favor pupils from the middle to upper classes, the majority of whom are white. Prof Pietersen observes that "the impoverished and vulnerable working classes, many of whom are black, make up the majority of South Africa's population. The pattern of favoring the upper and middle classes over the working class continues when children enrolled in universities go through the same social reproduction process". In Chapter 7 Prof Pietersen laments the perpetuation of socio-economic inequalities in the 'digital age'. He argues that while "optimal use of online or hybrid teaching platforms is critical to ensuring that higher education environments in developing universities should not be left behind . . . the very technology that enables online teaching and learning to take place in higher education is often the same factor that inhibits student success and limits teachers in their pedagogy". Chapter 8 grapples with the role of deliberative democracy in leading to pedagogies of dialogue and care in higher education online spaces., while Chapter 9 examined ways in which ODeL university instructors should improve the lives of students by inculcating qualities that can influence their futures by establishing a technologically stimulating online environment and crafting inclusive strategies to reach every student. In the 10th and concluding chapter, Prof Pietersen explores critical pedagogical action (specifically, dialogue and care) vis-à-vis the enactment of activism and justice among students in higher education. He seeks to make sense of theoretical understanding in the context of real pedagogical action in ODeL online university classrooms.

Twenty-five (25) years ago in 2000 I wrote that "Philosophizing involves getting clear about the meanings and uses of words, about the concepts that lie behind words, and about relevant types of reasons and arguments, so that serious issues may be discussed sensibly". I concluded that "Philosophizing is therefore a conceptual activity". As a lecturer of African philosophy of education at the University of Fort Hare at the time, which was, and continues to serve 100% African students from rural and disadvantaged parts of South Africa I put my head of the block by asserting that,

"The task of African philosophy is therefore to speculate about the communality of the individual in the African setting. It should provide conceptual frameworks for interpreting and analyzing the humanness that Botho and Ubuntu capture. It should provide rational tools for critical reflections on personal wellbeing or human flourishing, on communal ethics and how this ought to impact on human conduct"

In *Caring for Students Who Need It Most in Open Distance E-Learning Environments: This Is (Not) Hidden Philosophy*, Prof Pietersen not only engages in "philosophizing as a conceptual activity". He also engages in philosophy as provision of "rational tools for critical reflections on the culture of care and inclusion in ODeL, and how such critical reflection might engender personal wellbeing or human flourishing in communities and societies where rewards and opportunities to rise up the value chain are fundamentally skewed in favor of minority privileged classes.

Caring for Students Who Need It Most in Open Distance E-Learning Environments: This Is (Not) Hidden Philosophy is a timely and invaluable resource that is "a must read" for postgraduate students who are intent on carving their own research agendas in ODeL. I strongly recommend the book for academics, entry-level managers such as Heads of Departments (HOD), School Directors, College or Faculty Deans, Vice Principals for Directorates such as teaching, learning, and student support, student affairs, as well as research and innovation.

Foreword

Prof Moeketsi Letseka
Professor Extraordinaire
Distinguished Scholar and Distinguished Professor
Professor Emeritus: Chandigarh University, Uttar, Pradesh, India
Holder: UNESCO Chair on Open Distance Learning (ODL)
Member: South Africa's National Commission for UNESCO
Member: 15th Council of the National University of Lesotho (NUL)
Colleges of Education, and Graduate Studies
University of South Africa (UNISA)

Preface

One crucial question that arises in Open Distance e-Learning (ODeL) settings is how teachers may best support and nurture students who require the greatest help. The rapid growth of technology, such as the Fourth Industrial Revolution (4IR) and artificial intelligence (AI), has changed educational landscapes in the 21st century, making this question especially pertinent. Addressing the requirements of students who may encounter obstacles because of their socio-economic background, level of digital literacy or emotional health is difficult and calls for a thorough grasp of how to offer fair support in increasingly ODeL and digital environments.

Scholars in various educational contexts have asked this question, but not many researchers have begun to tackle this question by offering frameworks that emphasize holistic and inclusive approaches, especially when it comes to ODeL teaching and learning spaces. Edgar Morin's advocacy for transdisciplinary education highlights the importance of considering students' varied backgrounds and experiences, allowing for a more nuanced understanding of their needs. Other notable contributions in this field come from constructivist thinkers, such as Jonassen and Oduyoye, as well as wa Thiong'o who believe that fostering collaborative and learner-centered spaces can significantly enhance engagement and support for diverse student populations. Given this reality and the complexities introduced by AI and 4IR, a book addressing the care of students in ODeL is essential. It will not only synthesize existing scholarly insights, but also provide practical strategies for university educators to adapt and respond to the evolving educational demands of the digital age and ODeL contexts, ensuring that no student is left behind in this transformative era.

Acknowledgements

To every student in the past who has walked through my virtual classroom doors—whether hesitant, hopeful, or weary—your journeys have shaped the university educator I am today. I think of the undergraduate who bravely confessed, "I've never had someone believe in me before," and the postgraduate students who submitted their final work pieces with the note, "This is for everyone who said I wouldn't make it." Your struggles and triumphs are etched into these pages. You taught me that care is not an extra—it is the foundation.

To my current students, thank you for allowing me to walk alongside you. You are the reason this book exists *now*. This is not a research book, but a book that speaks to humanizing pedagogy foregrounded by the work of Paulo Freire. To the single parent balancing studies with night shifts, the first-generation student decoding academic jargon, the quiet thinker who only finds their voice in discussion forums. You remind me daily that pedagogy must adapt, that care is not static. My teaching has grown because of you—how I design flexibility into deadlines, how I listen for the unspoken struggles behind late submissions, how I now see my role not just as a facilitator of content, but as a guardian of possibility.

To my future students—know that this book is a pledge. I write with the humility of a university educator still learning, still transforming, and still wanting to care deeply. My promise to you is to keep questioning: *How can my pedagogy hold more space for your humanity? How can institutions like ours bend toward justice, not just efficiency?* This is not hidden philosophy—it is the visible work of showing up, again and again, even when systems make care feel like resistance.

To the colleagues who share this calling: may we never confuse rigor with rigidity, or metrics with meaning. And to my students— past, present, and future—thank you for trusting me with your stories. You are the reason "care" is not a footnote in education, but the text itself.

Professor Doniwen Pietersen

Abbreviations

ODeL	Online distance e-learning
LMS	Learning management system
COVID-19	Coronavirus disease of 2019
4IR	Fourth Industrial Revolution
UNISA	University of South Africa
AI	Artificial intelligence
PIF	Pietersen Intervention Framework

CHAPTER 1

Moving Towards a More Inclusive
and Caring ODeL Environments

Understanding these students will not only enable stakeholders to identify gaps in their knowledge and understanding of student financial support and its consequences for students, but also help universities create a more inclusive and supportive environment, improve student success and retention rates, and fulfill their broader social responsibilities.

—Otilia Chiramba and Elizabeth Sipiwe Ndofirepi

1. INTRODUCTION

Socio-economic inequality is pervasive in South African society and higher education is not exempt. This means that the lecturer's role is crucial in reducing inequality and building thoughtful, caring learning spaces, although this is not an easy assignment.[1] Inequality manifests in significant disparities in access to educational resources, quality of instruction, and student support

---

1. Ngwenya, *Disruption of Higher Education*, 36; Waghid, "Philosophy of Education," 1099–112.

services.[2] The South African higher education landscape reflects a complex interplay of historical injustices and contemporary socio-economic challenges where students from disadvantaged backgrounds often face barriers that hinder their academic success.[3] This context necessitates a critical examination of the role of lecturers in addressing these inequalities, particularly in Open Distance e-Learning (ODeL) environments where the potential for inclusivity and accessibility can be maximized.

2. CARING OPEN DISTANCE e-LEARNING SPACES IMPACT STUDENT SUCCESS

Lecturers play a crucial role in mitigating the effects of socio-economic inequality by creating thoughtful and caring learning spaces within ODeL frameworks.[4] Their responsibilities extend beyond content delivery; they must cultivate an environment that recognizes and addresses the diverse needs of students. This involves designing inclusive curricula, employing pedagogical strategies that promote engagement, and providing adequate support tailored to students' varying socioeconomic circumstances.[5] However, this task is not without its challenges. Many lecturers may lack the training or resources necessary to implement these strategies effectively, while systemic issues within institutions can hinder efforts to create equitable learning environments.[6] The success of these initiatives depends on a commitment to continuous improvement and collaboration among educators, administrators, and students.

Furthermore, building caring ODeL learning spaces is essential for fostering a sense of belonging and agency among students,

---

2. Shi and Sercombe, "Poverty and Inequality," 1–28.

3. Morrow, *Learning to Teach*, 220.

4. Baker et al., *COVID-19 Online Learning Landscapes*, 10.

5. Havergal, *Why Lecturers Must Take Responsibility*, 5.

6. Bazana and Mogotsi, "Social Identity and Racial Integration," 25; Hlatshwayo and Fomunyam, "Theorising #MustFall Student Movements," 61–80.

particularly those from disadvantaged backgrounds.[7] By prioritizing empathy and understanding, lecturers can create supportive networks that encourage students to engage actively in their education, thereby enhancing their academic outcomes.[8] This approach not only addresses immediate educational challenges, but also contributes to the broader goal of social justice in South Africa.[9] In essence, while the lecturer's role in reducing inequality and fostering caring learning environments is undeniably complex, it is also vital for transforming higher education into a more equitable space that empowers all students to succeed, irrespective of their socioeconomic backgrounds.[10]

Analyzing democracy in online higher education will therefore shed light on how ODeL institutions can effectively adapt to the dynamically shifting internal and external dynamics of learning and teaching. The significance of caring for students in ODeL environments will reveal how lecturers can involve students in the higher education learning environment in a culturally, socially, psychologically, and even politically engaging way, setting them up to succeed in their studies.[11]

3. Critical Dialogical Pedagogy in Open Distance e-Learning Education

In an online teaching and learning context, a lack of involvement between the lecturer and student remains an ongoing challenge.[12] Due to the fact that it appears to be a problem in higher education institutions, this issue allows for the formulation of the critical dialogical pedagogy of care. In ODeL contexts, the lack of involvement

7. Pendergast, "Engaging Marginalized Students," 138.

8. Mahlangu, "Creating Caring Learning Environments," 1–15.

9. Tjabane and Pillay, "Doing Justice to Social Justice," 10–8.

10. Shanyanana and Waghid, "Re-Imagined Notion of University Education," 1376–97.

11. Joorst, "Ethics of Care in Education," 127; Pietersen, "Engaging Paulo Freire," 211.

12. Le Roux, "Juggling Access vs Retention," 176–95.

between lecturers and students poses significant challenges to effective teaching and learning.[13] This disconnect can lead to feelings of isolation among students, which negatively impacts their engagement and academic performance. For instance, students may struggle to seek help or clarification on course materials when they feel disconnected from their lecturers, resulting in lower retention rates and diminished learning outcomes.[14] A practical example of this can be seen in online discussion forums where students may hesitate to participate due to a perceived lack of responsiveness from their lecturers, leading to a one-sided learning experience that fails to foster critical thinking and collaboration.[15]

To address this issue, the formulation of a critical dialogical pedagogy of care becomes essential. This pedagogical approach emphasizes the importance of dialogue and interaction between lecturers and students, fostering a supportive learning environment that prioritizes student well-being and engagement.[16] For example, lecturers can implement regular virtual office hours where students can engage in informal discussions about course content, share their thoughts, and ask questions. This practice not only enhances student involvement, but also builds rapport and trust, encouraging students to take an active role in their learning.[17] Additionally, incorporating collaborative projects that require students to work together can further enhance interaction and create a sense of community, which is often lacking in ODeL settings.[18]

Moreover, the critical dialogical pedagogy of care advocates for a reflective practice among educators, urging them to consider the sociocultural contexts of their students. By understanding

13. Pretorius, "Creating Context for Campus Sustainability," 530–47; Singh et al., "Students' Preferable Learning Mode," 1–8.

14. Nahal, "Voices from the Field", 1; Stough and Montague, "How Teachers Learn," 446–58.

15. García-Carrión, "Social Impact of Dialogic Teaching," 1–11.

16. Cassandra, "Enacting Dialogic Pedogogy," 1–23.

17. Gray and DiLoreto, "Effects of Student Engagement," n.p.; Sato et al., "Navigating the New Normal," 19.

18. Asterhan et al., "Controversies and Consensus," 1–16.

the diverse backgrounds and challenges faced by their students, lecturers can tailor their approaches to meet individual needs effectively.[19] For instance, a lecturer might use culturally relevant examples in their teaching materials or provide additional resources for students who may be struggling due to socioeconomic factors.[20] This approach not only promotes inclusivity, but also empowers students by validating their experiences and perspectives, ultimately leading to more engaged and motivated learners in ODeL environments.[21]

The type of online interaction between a lecturer and student calls for a connection that should be based on a care ethic that encourages dialogue. Unfortunately, there is a dearth of research that provides proof of the scope and efficacy of caring learning facilitation in ODeL institutions.[22] Such research would assist in fostering students to master independent and self-directed learning in order to succeed academically and become active citizens.[23] In light of these considerations, the following research question will uncover whether caring for students in ODeL environments from a deliberative democracy perspective ultimately leads to pedagogies of dialogue and care.

4. Caring Environments for Disadvantaged Students in Open Distance e-Learning Spaces

This study is based on recent research done by the South African Council on Higher Education which interrogates the state of caring for needy students from different perspectives. It posits that employing more caring and deliberative care will lead to positive democracy in ODeL institutions.[24] Students from disadvantaged

19. Chan and Hu, "Students' Voices on Generative AI," 43.

20. Maringe and Sing, "Teaching Large Classes," 761–82; Altes et al., *Challenges for Inclusion*, 2.

21. Jean-François, *Transnational Perspectives*, 5–10.

22. Kızılcık and Türüdü, "Humanising Online Teaching," 143–59.

23. Adinda and Mohib, "Instructional Design Approaches," 162–74.

24. Walker et al., *Low-Income Students*, 75.

backgrounds often face unique challenges that can hinder their academic success, such as limited access to technology, financial constraints, and inadequate support systems. To address these issues, ODeL institutions must adopt a more caring and deliberative approach that prioritizes the needs of these students.[25] For instance, institutions can implement targeted financial aid programs that not only alleviate tuition costs, but also provide stipends for essential resources, such as internet access and study materials. Such initiatives demonstrate a commitment to supporting needy students and can significantly enhance their educational experiences, ultimately contributing to a more equitable learning environment.[26]

Fostering a culture of care within ODeL institutions can lead to positive democratic outcomes by encouraging active participation and engagement among all students. When educators and administrators prioritize the well-being of their students, they create an environment where individuals feel valued and empowered to voice their opinions.[27] For example, institutions can establish student advisory boards that include representatives from diverse backgrounds, allowing them to contribute to decision-making processes regarding curriculum development and student support services.[28] This participatory approach not only enhances the sense of belonging among students, but also cultivates a democratic ethos within the institution where every voice is heard and respected.[29] Such practices align with the principles of critical dialogical pedagogy, which emphasize the importance of dialogue and collaboration in the learning process.[30]

Another way to look at this is to implement mentorship programs which can further enhance the caring framework within ODeL institutions, providing needy students with the guidance

---

25. Drury et al., *Assessing Deliberative Pedagogy*, 3.

26. Bastos, *Promoting Civic Engagement*, 10.

27. Bowden et al., "Four Pillars," 1207–24.

28. Pope et al., *Multicultural Competence*, 3.

29. Cook-Sather, "Respecting Voices," 885–901.

30. Englund, "Democratic Potential of the University," 281–7.

and support they require to navigate their educational journeys.[31] By pairing students with mentors who understand their specific challenges, institutions can facilitate meaningful connections that promote their academic success and personal growth. For instance, a mentorship program could involve experienced students or faculty members who offer regular check-ins, academic advice, and emotional support. This not only helps to bridge the gap between students and faculty, but also fosters a sense of community and solidarity among students.[32] Ultimately, by embracing a more caring and deliberative approach, ODeL institutions can create a supportive environment that empowers needy students and contributes to the development of a positive, democratic culture. This is reinforced by the recent work of scholars[33] who examine whether or not the online Learning Management System (LMS), much favored by higher education institutions, should become the new normal.

5. Dialogue Between Students and Lecturers in Open Distance e-Learning Spaces

These are worthwhile studies to take into account because they highlight the significance of higher education institutions moving toward a fully online teaching and learning environment.[34] From Freire's critical pedagogy,[35] it can be understood that teaching should inspire students to evaluate power structures and social injustice. The model of education he espoused encouraged an active dialogue between lecturer and student, so that the divide between the two dissolved and both learned alongside each other, resulting in equality and freedom from oppression.[36] Moreover, critical

---

31. Winthrop, *Need for Civic Education*, 5.

32. De Klerk, "Academic Advising," 152–68.

33. Gqokonqana et al., "Blended Learning Challenges," 87–107; Badaru and Adu, "Platformisation of Education," 66–86.

34. Skakane et al., "Providing Student Support," 97–114.

35. Freire, *Pedagogy of the Oppressed*, 13.

36. Richardson and Langford, "Care-Full Pedagogy," 408–20.

pedagogy stimulates students' thinking about social injustice to shift from mere theory to concerted action.[37]

In order to promote student growth, this study seeks to approach online teaching and learning from a compassionate and dialogical perspective.[38] By using democratic learning principles, such as thinking, expression, and opportunity, the dialogical and compassionate method enables students to exhibit an awareness of the world as a whole and as a collection of related systems.[39] Democracy is used in the teaching and learning process,[40] which improves both students' awareness and the connection between students and lecturers.[41] A more inclusive and caring philosophy can be expressed in the following way:

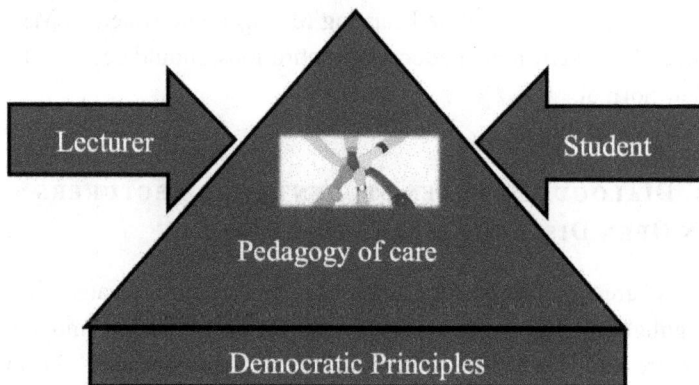

Figure 1. OdeL Transition to a More Caring and Inclusive Environment

This dynamic is visually represented by the above triangle, with the vertices symbolizing students, lecturers, and democratic principles. The connections between these points illustrate the

37. Stronach, "Ontario's Pedagogy of Oppression," 32–50.
38. Jansen, "Image-ing Teachers", 243–45.
39. Kumar and Downey, "Teaching as Meditative Inquiry," 52–75.
40. Dombaycı, "Philosophy for Children," 85–101.
41. Darder et al., "Critical Pedagogy," 1–30.

interplay of awareness, inclusivity, and care that underpins an effective learning environment.

Higher education should take into account the appropriation of the democratization of students' learning to converse with their professors while using a web-based LMS.[42] As a result, by recognizing the material they have acquired in their courses and their lecturers' sympathetic teaching, students will be able to show that they have a comprehension of the universe as a whole and as a collection of related systems. As they grow conscious of their involvement in the educational process,[43] students will be better able to express their unique personalities and advance intellectually.

6. CONCLUSION

Before scholarship becomes necessary, democratization of education necessitates a mutually beneficial relationship of cooperation, shared accountability, and justice. It should also be backed up by efficacy and relevance. Regretfully, not all instructors take a forward-thinking stance when it comes to their online teaching and learning assignments. To teach pupils how to be good citizens, this must be addressed in order to equalize educational chances, liberty, and kinship. It is the duty of lecturers to democratically involve students in the online teaching and learning process. This is the ultimate goal of all levels of schooling.

42. Jansen, "Image-ing Teachers," 243–45; Mncube, *Domestication of Open Educational Resources*, 16–20.

43. Jeffrey and Craft, "Teaching Creatively," 77–87.

CHAPTER 2

Caring from a Democratic Perspective and the Engagement Of Students in ODeL Environments

Care for students exceeds merely providing content and designing learning activities. In their view, such care acknowledges each student's existence as a human being with needs and aspirations, which necessitates a closer look than before at the connection between care and online student engagement.

—Thembeka Shange

1. INTRODUCTION

Going online is the new norm for higher education. The external environment, including the Fourth Industrial Revolution (4IR), COVID 19, and the uncertain learning environment, has had an impact on education as a whole.[1] The use of a learning management system (LMS), such as Moodle, Blackboard, and others, must be done in an inclusive way from a dialogical and care point of view, underscoring the significance of deliberative democracy.[2] The issue of democracy in higher online education will therefore

---

1. Whalley et al., "Flexible Personalized Learning," 79–99.
2. Shaffer and Longo, *Creating Space for Democracy*, 9.

shed light on how open distance institutions of higher learning and teaching can effectively adapt to the dynamically shifting internal and external dynamics of learning and teaching.[3] Answering this question will clarify how lecturers should engage with students in higher education to support their academic success.[4]

This book reflects philosophical and dialogical pedagogies from the perspective of deliberative democracy in online higher education,[5] which relates to caring for students who need it most in an ODeL environment. Particularly in open distance e-Learning (ODeL) environments, philosophical and dialogical pedagogies rooted in deliberative democracy play a crucial role in fostering an inclusive and caring educational atmosphere (Farooq, 2019). Deliberative democracy emphasizes the importance of dialogue and collective reasoning,[6] which aligns with the principles of philosophical pedagogy that advocate for critical thinking and reflective engagement among students. By creating spaces where students can voice their concerns and contribute to discussions,[7] educators can cultivate a sense of belonging and agency, particularly for those who may be marginalized or in need of additional support.[8] This approach not only enhances the learning experience, but also empowers students to become active participants in their educational journey, thereby promoting social justice and equity in access to education.[9]

The application of dialogical pedagogies in ODeL settings encourages a collaborative learning environment where students are seen as co-creators of knowledge, rather than passive recipients.[10] This shift is particularly significant for students who require more

3. Ramirez et al., "All-Learning," 944–53.

4. Garrison and Kanuka, "Blended Learning," 95–105; Cele et al., "African Student's Social Identities," 240–51.

5. Gutmann and Thompson, *Why Deliberative Democracy*, 21.

6. Wegerif, *Dialogic*, 20; Alexander, *Dialogic Teaching Companion*, 100.

7. Noddings, "Caring Relation in Teaching," 771–81.

8. Pietersen and Plaatjies, "Freirean Utopian Didactic," 123–37.

9. Pietersen, "Engaging Paulo Freire," 211.

10. Sulé et al., "Case for Case Studies," 321–36.

care and attention, as it allows for personalized learning experiences that cater to diverse needs. Educators can facilitate meaningful interactions through various online platforms, ensuring that all voices are heard and valued.[11] By integrating philosophical inquiry into the curriculum, educators can challenge students to reflect on their values and beliefs, fostering a deeper understanding of their roles within a democratic society. Ultimately, this pedagogical approach not only addresses the immediate educational needs of students, but also prepares them to engage thoughtfully and responsibly in their communities.[12] Creating pedagogical caring communities is an attempt to enhance better instruction and learning by opening up the online classroom to more students and lecturers. This benefit does not, however, preclude significant advantages for graduates at higher education institutions like developing universities.[13]

2. LEARNING AND ENGAGEMENT IN OPEN DISTANCE E-LEARNING

According to research done by South Africa's Council on Higher Education (CHE), great challenges exist in online higher education, specifically when it comes to the engagement between lecturer and student. The report emphasizes the importance of rethinking student engagement in the learning process—including in ODeL environments—and highlights the need to unlearn ingrained habits developed over years of experience. Teaching and learning are somewhat influenced by technology, according to many reports on Higher education institutions in Africa. Philosophical and dialogical pedagogies within the framework of deliberative democracy are increasingly relevant in online higher education, particularly in ODeL environments. These pedagogies advocate for a model of education that prioritizes dialogue, critical

11. Shemshack and Spector, "Personalized Learning Terms," 33.
12. Pietersen, "Engaging Paulo Freire," 211.
13. Sanger, "Inclusive Pedagogy," 31–71.

thinking, and collective engagement among students. Deliberative democracy emphasizes the importance of discourse in decision-making processes, suggesting that when students are encouraged to express their perspectives,[14] they become active participants in their learning.[15] This is particularly vital for students who may be marginalized or require additional support, as the dialogical approach fosters a sense of community and belonging.[16] By creating a supportive online environment, educators can address the unique challenges faced by these students, ultimately enhancing their educational experiences and outcomes.[17]

Incorporating technology into teaching and learning practices in ODeL settings allows for innovative methods of engagement that align with philosophical and dialogical pedagogies.[18] Online platforms provide diverse tools for interaction—such as discussion forums, video conferencing, and collaborative projects—that can facilitate meaningful dialogue among students.[19] These technologies enable educators to create spaces where students can share their thoughts and experiences, thus promoting a culture of mutual respect and understanding. Moreover, technology can help bridge gaps for students who may struggle with traditional learning methods, allowing for personalized and flexible learning experiences. This adaptability is crucial in caring for students who need it most, as it enables tailored support that meets diverse learning needs.[20]

The integration of deliberative democracy principles into online education encourages students to engage critically with their learning materials and with one another. By fostering an environment where students can deliberate on ethical issues and

---

14. Maurissen et al., "Deliberation in Citizenship Education," 951–72.

15. Garrison and Anderson, *E-Learning*, 10.

16. Beckett et al., "Beyond Inclusion," 132.

17. Ferri et al., "Online Learning," 86.

18. Peterson et al., *Understanding Innovative Pedagogies*, 11–12.

19. Moore, *Distance Education*, 18–20; McNeil et al., "Facilitating Interaction," 699–708.

20. Alam and Mohanty, "Educational Technology," 2283282.

societal challenges,[21] educators not only enhance critical thinking skills, but also prepare students to become responsible citizens in a democratic society.[22] This educational approach is particularly important in an era where technology shapes both communication and learning modalities. As students navigate online spaces, the ability to engage thoughtfully in discussions and to consider multiple viewpoints becomes essential.[23] Ultimately, the philosophical and dialogical pedagogies grounded in deliberative democracy not only support the academic growth of students, but also contribute to their holistic development as empathetic and informed individuals in a rapidly changing world.[24]

3. Caring for Students in Open Distance e-Learning

There are various levels of engagement needed if we start to care for students in ODeL spaces. However, most of the challenges seem to be focused on technological issues and not necessarily on student engagement.[25] This is supported by scholars[26] in their investigations around how the online LMS ought to be the new normal.

Caring for students who need it most in ODeL environments is a multifaceted challenge that necessitates a thoughtful integration of pedagogical principles and technological tools.[27] In this context, philosophical perspectives on care emphasize the moral responsibility of educators to create inclusive and supportive learning environments.[28] The notion of care in education is rooted

---

21. Pietersen et al., "Techno-Rationalism," 163–78.

22. Bailin and Battersby, *Critical Thinking*, 12.

23. Whiteside et al., *Social Presence in Online Learning*, 20.

24. Devine, "Socratic Circles Pedagogy," 1053–69; Hoch, "Intercultural Dialogues," 59–88.

25. Bond et al., "Student Engagement and Educational Technology," 1–30.

26. Gqokonqana et al., "Blended Learning Challenges," 87-107; Badaru and Adu, "Platformisation of Education," 66–86.

27. Modise, *Empathetic Student Support*, 20–31.

28. Buchanan et al., "Philosophy of Education," 1178–97.

in the belief that all students, particularly those from marginalized backgrounds, deserve equitable access to learning opportunities.[29] This care-oriented approach aligns with the principles of ODeL, where flexibility and accessibility are paramount. By prioritizing the needs of vulnerable students, educators can foster a sense of belonging and agency, which are critical for student success in online and ODeL settings.[30]

The implementation of an LMS as the new normal in ODeL environments serves as a vital mechanism for enhancing care and support for students. LMS platforms are designed to facilitate communication, collaboration,[31] and resource sharing, thereby creating a virtual space where students can engage meaningfully with course content and with one another.[32] From a philosophical standpoint, the use of an LMS aligns with the dialogical approach to education, which values the exchange of ideas and perspectives among learners.[33] By utilizing features like discussion forums, quizzes, and personalized learning paths, educators can tailor the learning experience to meet the diverse needs of students, ensuring that those who require additional support receive the attention they need to thrive.

The role of LMS in ODeL environments extends beyond mere content delivery; it embodies a commitment to fostering a culture of care and responsiveness.[34] Educational institutions must recognize that the effectiveness of a LMS hinges on its ability to adapt to the unique needs of students.[35] This includes incorporating feedback mechanisms, providing timely support services, and ensuring that the platform is user-friendly and accessible to all learners.[36] By embracing these principles, educators not only

---

29. Noddings, *Moral and Character Education*, 188.

30. Al Amri, *Integrating Care Pedagogy*, 31.

31. Sato, et al., "Navigating the New Normal," 19.

32. Langegård, "Nursing Students' Experiences," 1–10.

33. Garrison and Anderson, *E-Learning*, 8.

34. Grimes, "Enhancing Online Learners' Experiences," 167–94.

35. Sershan et al., "Transformative Role of Academics," 164–78.

36. Moore, *Distance Education*, 35.

enhance the academic experience, but also promote a holistic approach to student welfare that is essential for nurturing resilient and engaged learners.[37] Ultimately, the integration of a LMS into an ODeL environment represents a philosophical commitment to caring for all students, reaffirming the notion that education should be a collaborative journey, rather than a solitary endeavor.[38]

These studies are valuable as they underscore the importance of higher education institutions transitioning to fully online teaching and learning. However, what they overlook—and what this researcher contends—is that activism and justice in higher education cannot be realized through theory alone, but must be enacted through meaningful pedagogical practices in the classroom.[39] Moreover, an amendment to Freire's notion of dialogical engagement extends to deliberative action. Freire himself was epistemologically concerned with dialogical action.[40] Together with his exploration of deliberative democratic theory, he offers a different way of looking at cultivating a socially just higher pedagogy.

4. Democratizing and Dialogical Caring within Open Distance e-Learning

Engagement with students in a democratic way offers profound positive consequences[41] if LMS platforms are used appropriately.[42] Approaching online teaching and learning from a caring and dialogical perspective in order to achieve student development is critically important. The caring and dialogical approach allows students to demonstrate an understanding of the world as a whole and as a set of related systems by applying democratic learning

37. Hill et al., "Pedagogic Partnership," 167–85.

38. Plueger, Lived Experiences, 39–60.

39. Kane and Dahlvig, "Traditional Faculty Resistance," 1–16.

40. Liambas and Kaskaris, "Dialogue and Love," 185–96; Armonda, *In Freire More than Freire*, 93–126.

41. Wood et al., "Pedagogies for Active Citizenship," 259–67.

42. Gqokonqana et al., "Blended Learning Challenges," 87-107.

principles such as thought, expression, and opportunity.[43] The use of democracy in the teaching and learning process not only enhances the student-lecturer relationship, but also benefits students further afield.[44]

The effective use of an LMS in higher education ought to consider the appropriation of the democratization of students' learning to dialogue with their lecturers.[45] This will allow students to demonstrate an understanding of the world as a whole and as a set of related systems by recognizing the content learned in their courses through the lens of their lecturer's empathy. Students will be able to display their individual personality and develop academically as they become aware of their role in the education process.[46] Preceding the need for scholarship, democratizing education involves a reciprocal relationship of cooperation, shared responsibility, and justice.

As students become aware of their roles in the educational process, they are better positioned to display their individual personalities and foster their academic development.[47] This awareness empowers them to take ownership of their learning experiences, enabling them to express their unique perspectives and engage deeply with course content. When students recognize that their contributions are valued, they are more likely to participate actively, collaborate with peers, and form meaningful connections with the learning community.[48] This active engagement not only enhances their academic skills, but also allows students to cultivate their identities in a supportive environment where authenticity

---

43. Dewey, *Democracy and Education*, xxxix-xl.

44. Van der Westhuijzen, *Taking Art Out of the Classroom*, 16–39.

45. Jansen, "Image-ing Teachers," 243–45; Rhoads et al., "Open Courseware Movement," 87–110.

46. Tinto, "Classrooms as Communities," 599–623; Aina et al., "Determinants of University Dropout," 101102.

47. Kuh, "Other Curriculum," 123–55; Groccia, "Student Engagement," 11–20.

48. Kooy, "Collaborative Teaching," 187–209; Sherman, *Learning Community Implementation*, 30–40.

and diverse viewpoints are celebrated.[49] Consequently, this dynamic promotes a culture of care[50] as students feel encouraged to share their thoughts and experiences without fear of judgment.

5. Caring, Shared Responsibility, and Justice in Open Distance e-Learning

The democratization of education is fundamentally rooted in the principles of cooperation, shared responsibility, and justice.[51] When educational environments prioritize these values, they create a reciprocal relationship between educators and students.[52] In this context, educators act not only as facilitators of knowledge, but also as supporters and mentors who guide students in recognizing the significance of their roles in the learning process.[53] This relationship fosters a sense of collective ownership over the educational experience where students feel empowered to contribute to discussions and collaborate on projects.[54] Such interactions cultivate a climate of mutual respect and understanding, reinforcing the notion that education is a shared journey rather than a solitary endeavor.

Furthermore, fostering a culture of care and shared responsibility in education directly contributes to the development of social justice.[55] When students are encouraged to express themselves and take an active role in their learning, they also become more aware of the diverse needs and perspectives within their educational community.[56] This awareness cultivates empathy and

49. Noddings, *Moral and Character Education*, 95–100.

50. Kreber, "Teacher Identities," 171–94.

51. Sahlberg, "Rethinking Accountability," 45–61.

52. Demirbolat, *Democracy and Education*, 70–80.

53. Garrison and Anderson, *E-Learning*, 20.

54. Purkarthofer, Eva, and Raine Mäntysalo, "Collaborative Student-Led Learning," 1148–159.

55. Maguire and Lenihan, "Social Justice in Art Education," 39–53; Keifer-Boyd, *Social Justice Art Education*, 20–35.

56. McCaleb, *Building Communities of Learners*, 215.

solidarity among students, prompting them to advocate for one another and contribute to an inclusive learning environment.[57] By democratizing education through a framework that emphasizes cooperation and justice, institutions not only enhance academic outcomes, but also prepare students to be responsible citizens who value diversity and actively work towards equity in their communities.[58] Ultimately, this holistic approach to education nurtures both individual growth and collective well-being, reinforcing the idea that caring for students is essential for fostering a vibrant and just educational landscape.

6. Conclusion

This study is positioned against the modification of Freire's pedagogy, specifically the extension of the concept of dialogical engagement to pedagogies of caring and deliberative action. In order to achieve equality of educational opportunities and to teach students how to be good citizens, lecturers in ODeL environments should ensure that students are involved in the online teaching process. They should also be able to identify students who are not progressing in the execution of their online learning tasks. In all forms of education, this is the ultimate objective. This objective aligns with the development of critical pedagogical action in relation to the implementation of justice and activism in ODeL university classrooms.

57. Moore, *Distance Education*, 130.

58. Benson et al., *Dewey's Dream*, 20–24; Albulescu and Simut, "Developing Democratic Citizens," 167–87.

CHAPTER 3

Dialogue and Care for Students in ODeL Environments

The lecturer's voice dominates over students' meaning-making voices, it becomes a barrier to effective dialogue in the [online] classroom, consequently reinforcing the lecturer-student power dynamic.

—Daniela Rothwell

1. INTRODUCTION

An effective education system is one where students feel cared for, included, and are able to deliver critical dialogical input in their learning, including in ODeL environments.[1] This chapter aims to epitomize quality education of dialogue and care where skills, values, and equal distribution of resources can be accessed by all. This includes effectively trained lecturers who manage diversity and teach effectively to foster success and provide a safe and friendly classroom environment for students. This chapter focuses on how to administer clear dialogical and caring aims in online higher education spaces where students can grow holistically and

---

1. Karam, "Re-envisioning the ESOL Classroom," e582; Kızıldağ[set breve over g] and Kaçar, "Toward More Inclusive Classroom Practices," 147.

critically.[2] It addresses the kind of space lecturers need to create online to offer students the opportunity to be part of a caring teaching and learning process in order to form part of an active citizenry beyond their immediate context.[3]

In addition, this chapter emphasizes how Freire's dialogical theory regarding online higher education can be transformed to facilitate student success and create engagement in student-lecturer relations. The contribution lies in applying Freire's pedagogical framework and extending it through the book's concept of dialogical engagement, ultimately connecting it to deliberative caring action in ODeL spaces to support holistic student growth.

2. Enhance Student Engagement in Open Distance e-Learning

Several factors have affected university students in recent years, including those at developing universities. These factors include the Fourth Industrial Revolution, the COVID 19 pandemic, and the uncertain learning and teaching environment.[4] Using LMS platforms, such as Blackboard, and involving students with a need to critically engage with the world around them could positively impact their academic success. According to Loots,[5] most individuals would agree that academic performance isn't the only factor in student success. It has to do with the qualities, information, and abilities that students acquire while enrolled in college. It also has to do with how applicable these elements are to the real world of today and tomorrow. In addition, due to the country's sociopolitical past, South Africa has a sense of social justice, which is demonstrated by the desire to reduce achievement inequalities,

---

2. Gordon, "Trusting Students' Voices," 1–32.

3. Caetano, "Student Voice and Participation," 57–73.

4. Mhlanga, "Introducing Blended Learning," 15; Mhlanga et al., "Key Digital Transformation Lessons," 464.

5. Loots, *Mapping UFS Students' Journeys*, 8–9.

broaden access, and concentrate on creating critical, democratic citizens.[6]

Discussions of this kind can provide insights into how faculties at higher learning institutions can respond more effectively to the ever-changing external and internal worlds of learning and teaching.[7] All staff members must have a deep awareness of and compassion for their students' educational experiences. Lecturers may even be able to use these insights to engage students socially and psychologically, so that they can thrive in their studies. Without a doubt, instructors can create an environment where students feel intellectually supported, know how to access help, navigate institutional rules, and stay informed about the latest and most exciting developments in the field. Behind-the-scenes support systems for instructors and students are frequently created and maintained by the village of administrative and support personnel. In a recent study, students acknowledged the importance of both academic and extracurricular support networks that enabled them to thrive.[8]

The chapter explores how well-trained lecturers can navigate a pedagogy of dialogue and care by teaching effectively, evaluating their LMS competencies, upholding shared values, and ensuring the equitable distribution of resources in the teaching and learning process.[9] Aside from ensuring a safe and friendly learning environment, the goal is to facilitate the success of students. This chapter also discusses the possibility of providing students with dialogue and care that provides a learning experience which encourages students to become active citizens. The methodological framework and the theoretical frameworks of Freire and others will

6. Vally, "Pedagogy of Possibility," 1–24; Sinwell, "Communities of Struggle," 1–19.

7. Kezar, *New Concepts for Higher Education*, 1999–2000; Holcombe, *Shared Leadership in Higher Education*, 5–7.

8. Ndofirepi, *Rethinking Social Spaces*, 143; Maringe et al., *Clash of Ideologies*, 145–157.

9. Srinivasa and Siddesh, *Confluence of Teaching and Learning*, 1–20.

be discussed. Afterwards, the chapter will describe the proposed teaching approaches and conclude with some recommendations.

3. Critical Consciousness in Open Distance e-Learning

Brazilian educationalist and philosopher Paulo Freire's methodology is strongly shaped by a theological frame of reference situated in a caring and critical pedagogy, particularly in his reflections on teaching and learning environments.[10] His theory of dialogue in educational contexts can be summarized as the encounter between individuals, mediated by the world, through which they express it—not confined solely to the I-you relationship.[11]

Freire's (1972) modus operandi is a methodological approach that is effective, albeit not widespread. Following his strategy, the culture circle is used in which the teacher and student create reflections and discussions about reality and collectively seek to unveil and identify the possibilities of learning. The culture circle is a concept that speaks to the critical consciousness of inequities and addresses their causes and insists on transforming their social and political circumstances[12] as part of the learning process.[13]

The process lays bare how students positively and actively participate in an online learning process, even on ODeL platforms, where the stories of students and who they are as individuals from different backgrounds lend richness to the learning and teaching process.[14] This ultimately allows all stakeholders in the learning and teaching process to strengthen and modify these practices.[15]

---

10. Hazelton and Haigh, "Incorporating Sustainability into Accounting Curricula," 159–78; Tavares, *Century of Paulo Freire*, 150.

11. Freire, *Pedagogy of the Oppressed*, 10; Heidemann and Almeida, "Friere's Dialogic Concept," 159–67.

12. Zulu, "Struggles and Triumphs," 252.

13. Hlatshwayo and Fomunyam, "Theorising #MustFall Student Movements," 61–80.

14. Longo, "Deliberative Pedagogy," 1–18.

15. Davids and Waghid, *Democratic Citizenship Education*, 224.

Freire's methodology is an approach that encourages a reflective process where both lecturers and students are able to value the cultural and historical sources of individuals, which can be revealed in culture circles which Davids and Waghid[16] refer to as active citizenry. Through the journey mapping project of Loots (2021), the entire educational journey of developing university students in ODeL has been examined—from their first interaction with the university, including ODeL environments, to getting ready to transition out of university and into the world of work or pursuing postgraduate qualifications. Such an analysis allows us to see which aspects contribute to students' success, at which times, and how these factors interact with each other. This, in turn, enables developing universities to align their curricular and co-curricular initiatives with students' experiences[17] which includes not only caring for students outside of assessments and content teaching, but also allowing them to be co-deliberators of learning and teaching initiatives online that have an impact on their success.

4. LECTURERS SUPPORT STUDENTS IN OPEN DISTANCE E-LEARNING

The teaching and learning processes of a transformative higher education institution, such as developing universities, are based on a system that aims to produce students who are able to identify, analyze, and solve everyday problems.[18] Students must be able to think critically and creatively, both inside and outside of their study discipline. Once they have completed their studies, they must be able to take responsibility for their own actions in life.[19] They must be able to manage themselves and their activities effectively and responsibly. In order to successfully develop, they must

16. Davids and Waghid, *Democratic Citizenship Education*, 226.

17. Lombard, "JuniorTukkie Program," 1–14.

18. Waghid, "Knowledge Production," 457–88; Nasim, "Total Quality Management," 75–97.

19. Cele et al., "African Student's Social Identities," 240–51.

be able to communicate well using language skills, either visual or symbolic.[20]

The efficient administration of instruction and learning in higher education must consider the appropriation of the democratization of students' learning to dialogue with their lecturers.[21] In so doing, students will be able to demonstrate an understanding of the world as a whole and as a set of related systems[22] by recognizing the content learned in their courses. Thus, the proper use of an LSM, such as Moodle and Blackboard, can be applied to the teaching and learning process, but also to how students should conduct themselves further afield.[23] This means that lecturers and an LMS should be viewed as critical tools in the development and growth of students from developing universities, in particular, to care for students in ODeL environments.

Moreover, a strong emphasis on the importance of making connections and having critical engagement between students and lecturers in higher education institutions plays a vital role in mediating students' expectations and learning experiences.[24] Many students agree that there is a lack of communication from lecturers, as well as frustrations with a general lack of interactive communication between students, lecturers, and peers.[25] Many students find it difficult to engage on online platforms with lecturers. This ultimately creates a culture of exclusion.[26]

20. Bloch, *Education Beyond Crisis*, 8; Pietersen and Dube, "African Students' Authorial Voice," 318–27.

21. Jansen, "Image-ing Teachers," 243–45; Alyoussef, "Massive Open Online Courses," 531.

22. Mashiyi, *Old History Textbooks*, 13–20.

23. Maluleke, "Usage of Blackboard Learn," 39–62.

24. Gravett and Winstone, "Making Connections," 360–74.

25. Wallace, "Online Learning," 241–80; Baloran, "Course Satisfaction and Student Engagement," 1–12.

26. Mehta and Aguilera, "Humanizing Pedagogies," 109–20; Karakose, "Emergency Remote Teaching," 53–61.

5. INTERSECTION OF CARE AND CRITICAL PEDAGOGY IN OPEN DISTANCE E-LEARNING

The concepts of dialogical and critical engagement, as well as socially just pedagogies, form part of the overall care needed for students in an ODeL environment. It is important to know that in an ODeL environment, dialogue in caring for students cannot be boiled down to a single person sharing ideas with another or a discussion in which participants merely absorb ideas.[27] According to Freire, educators and facilitators cannot simply consider themselves as people who force their opinions on those who are less educated or are passive recipients of information waiting to digest it unquestioningly. This would deliberately ignore the voices of students.[28] This should never be the case, even if it means drawing students out of their comfort zones.[29] It can be expressed in the following way:

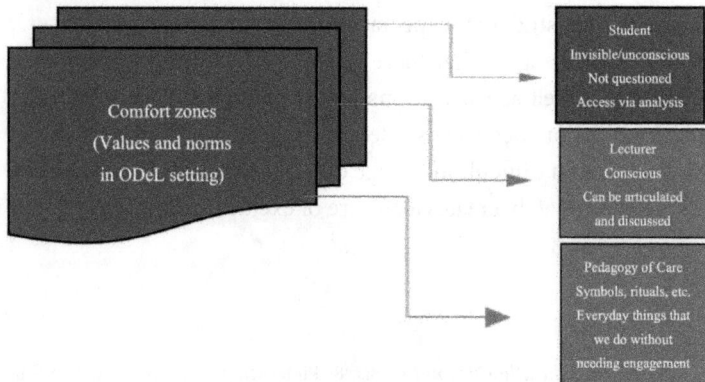

Figure 2. Prioritizing Dialogue and Care-Driven Teaching and Learning Approaches in ODeL

Prioritizing dialogue and care-driven teaching and learning approaches in Open and Distance e-Learning (ODeL) settings

27. Dewey, *Democracy and Education*, xxii.
28. Darder et al., "Critical Pedagogy," 1–30.
29. Freire, *Pedagogy of Freedom*, 36; Bovill, Relational Pedagogy, 1967.

necessitates a deliberate shift from traditional pedagogical norms to practices that foster inclusivity, empathy, and engagement.[30] In ODeL environments, students often operate within invisible or unconscious comfort zones shaped by entrenched values and norms, which are rarely questioned or critically examined.[31] These comfort zones can hinder meaningful learning by perpetuating passive engagement and limiting access to deeper analytical understanding. Lecturers, as conscious facilitators, play a pivotal role in articulating and discussing these implicit boundaries, thereby creating spaces where students feel seen and valued.[32] A pedagogy of care, as advocated by American philosopher Nel Noddings,[33] emphasizes the importance of symbols, rituals, and everyday practices that cultivate a sense of belonging and mutual respect. By embedding care-driven approaches—such as regular check-ins, collaborative discussions, and reflective activities— educators can transform mundane routines into opportunities for meaningful engagement. This not only challenges the status quo, but also empowers students to critically engage with their learning environments, fostering a culture of care that transcends the virtual divide.[34] Lecturers need to swallow their pride and embrace tolerance in order to consider what reality looks like from their students' perspective. This is well expressed by Osler:

> . . . a strong emphasis on citizenship as feeling (student identities, with particular attention to national identity) and on citizenship as practice (active citizenship, engagement in the local community) [especially true for ODeL learning environments]. The new ways in which citizens can engage actively as citizens, across and beyond the boundaries of the nation, as a result of information technologies, are not explored, and so the emphasis on active citizenship or citizenship as practice remains largely

30. Sinha, *Reconfiguring Pedagogy*, 93–122.

31. Bozalek and Zembylas, "Diffraction or Reflection," 111–27.

32. Gravett et al., "Pedagogies of Mattering," 388–403.

33. Noddings, "Caring Relation in Teaching," 771–81.

34. Pietersen, "Engaging Paulo Freire," 211.

confined to the school [and ODeL institutions] and local communities.[35]

Freire emphasizes that without humility, it is difficult to listen respectfully to someone whom one perceives as being significantly less capable than oneself. However, it is imperative that the care lecturers have for their students be armed love, the battling love of people who believe that it is their duty and right to struggle, denounce, and announce. Lecturers must all learn this kind of love, which is essential to the progressive educator.[36] Another virtue is tolerance. Without it, no serious pedagogical work is possible, no authentic democratic experience is viable, and all progressive educational practice is denied, especially in ODeL environments.

6. Conclusion

In a caring ODeL environment, lecturers bear the responsibility of ensuring that all parties involved in the process of online education are included. They also need to be progressive in how they perform teaching and learning tasks on LMS platforms in ODeL contexts. In relation to the work of Freire and others, dialogical pedagogy is needed to frame the critical engagement of the teaching and learning process, and to care for students who need it most. In the ODeL environment, we need to be reminded that students, as well as lecturers, add value to the learning and teaching process of online distance learning, and all stakeholders' input must be considered of primary importance.

35. Osler, "Interpretations of Citizenship Education," 7.
36. Price, "Richness of Complexity," 42–53.

CHAPTER 4

Caring for Students and Being Deliberate About Teaching and Learning Approaches in ODeL Environments

The importance of a dialogical education is that it considers the contexts of students and provides them with theoretical and practical tools to face their reality. The discussion emphasizes the need to implement this pedagogy to foster critical consciousness and contribute to social improvement..

—Escobar et al.

1. INTRODUCTION

Teaching and learning in an ODeL environment needs to be based on caring for students who need it most. This an important part of the process of education. However, it is also measurable through which quality education can be standardized. According to Peters,[1] for proper education to take place, including ODeL platforms, being measurable must be central if teachers and facilitators are to be impactful. Peters suggests that education that is centered around caring for students in an ODeL environment

1. Peters, *Ethics and Education*, 251–55.

must include knowledge, comprehension, and some form of cognitive perspective, which are not inert, and that caring education entails the transmission of what is worthwhile to those who become dedicated to it, that certain transmission methods are at least excluded from education because pupils are not willing or voluntarily involved in them. Peters' view that it is critical for a lecturer to foreground the dialogical and deliberative pedagogies is noteworthy. He believes learning and education in general are transmitted by teachers and that these also translate into how prepared they are in the use of learning tools, such as Moodle and LMS platforms in general. Not only this, but how students perceive the actual use of such tools in the knowledge and understanding process is also crucial.

Moreover, Biesta highlights what the underlining antithesis to the teaching and learning process in an ODeL environment is.[2] He is of the view that since ODeL environments ultimately depend on the possibility of truth—more especially, truth free from power—both monological and dialogical methods are necessary. In the dialogical approach, this truth is discovered through the process of group learning, whereas in the lecturer's case, it is learnt from and so imparted. Since liberation is viewed as a process of overcoming ideological distortions, the monological method is predicated on the notion of truth that is untarnished by power. In this context, emancipation functions as a demythologizing process. Emancipation, or actual human praxis in Freirean terminology, is the process that restores genuine human existence according to the dialogical method.

The relationship between student and lecturer—and the ways in which they relate and collaborate throughout the learning process—requires careful consideration, particularly when power dynamics between them are unequal.[3] The attempt to achieve this can be summarized by Greene[4] when she asserts that "[teaching and learning is] joined to a justice or equity process". This process

2. Biesta, "Politics of Learning," 4–15.
3. Joorst, "Ethics of Care in Education," 6.
4. Greene, "Critical Pedagogy," 430.

ought to prompt students, as well as lecturers, to question meanings and ideas, to imagine alternative possibilities and outcomes, to modify practical judgements, and to develop respect and critical engagement in their field of study. In this way, critical assignation and deliberation is unhindered communicative liberty that involves both rational opinion and willful allowance of information which can almost always potentially lead to a transformation in people's preferences and perceptions of their learning.[5]

2. Ensuring Access and Equity for Students Open Distance e-Learning

Before continuing, it is important to justify why and how this chapter's research problem arises. In other words, what are the factors that contribute to the research problem? Because my experience is rooted in developing universities, I recognize that the research problem is embedded in a broader context—one in which many transforming higher education institutions, often unwittingly, remain part of an unevenly distributed education and training system that presents significant barriers to growth. It is my conviction that quality education ought to be evenly distributed and should be available to all South African students, regardless of their socioeconomic background. Many other transforming higher education institutions need to set equitable teaching and learning standards for their students. They also have the responsibility to create teaching and learning outcomes that are achievable as a means of empowering students to be part of their own learning process. According to Phejane,[6] online learning has been seamless at institutions such as developing universities. However, poor students encountered a number of obstacles to utilizing the full potential of online learning, including a lack of adequate data and internet connectivity.[7] And, when setting the content and

---

5. Adams and Waghid, "Deliberative Democracy," 28.
6. Phejane, "The New Normal," 164–78.
7. Phejane, "The New Normal," 164–78.

standards for teaching and learning on online platforms such as Blackboard, it should be kept in mind that all students need to develop to reach their full potential as persons, not just for academic brilliance, but also further afield.[8]

Factors that sustain excellent dialogical outcomes for a transformative higher education institution's teaching and learning plans ought to include the views of students, particularly when it comes to indigenous knowledge, as their views form part of their educational formation. If this is done well, students will feel that they have been included and this will create depth and meaning. Thus, higher education institutions would have wholly developed students that are both globally and locally engaged and who are not restricted by geographical borders.[9] This problematization can only be addressed by lecturers reviving the eventalization of the intentional emancipation of education.[10] In other words, it is not necessary in the ODeL caring space for criticism to be the starting point of a deduction that leads to this conclusion. It ought to be a tool for those who oppose, battle, and reject the status quo. It should be used in confrontational and conflictual activities, as well as in articles that express refusal. It is not required to establish the law for the sake of the law. It is not a programming stage. It is a challenge aimed at what already exists.

This discourse does not allow the possibility for any individual or group of students to be excluded from critical, dialogical, and deliberative educational matters that interest them and that determine their future; they are free to critically engage in the teaching and learning process. After all, the rights of students to participate in deliberative, critical, and dialogical engagement are legally institutionalized and should be measured against the effective use of teaching and learning tools. This means that each individual student has an equal opportunity to be heard during the deliberative and dialogical process,[11] which in turn means that

8. Bloch, *Education Beyond Crisis*, 9.

9. Bloch, *Education Beyond Crisis*, 10.

10. Foucault, "Questions of Method," 41.

11. Adams and Waghid, "Deliberative Democracy," 25–33.

the viewpoints of the minority are heard, while the domination of the majority is limited. However, in order for critical, dialogical engagement and deliberation to be effective and truly beneficial, certain aspects of the online teaching and learning process need to be constantly monitored by the lecturer.[12]

3. Transformative Power of Dialogical Consensus and Caring in Open Distance e-Learning

Jürgen Habermas offers great insights into the dialogical theory of deliberation. Juxtaposing Habermas with Freire sheds a unique light on the dialogical and deliberation pedagogies because both theorists foreground the role of transformative education. For Freire, the goal of caring education, including in ODeL environments, is to create well-read, considerate, scholarly people with a strong ability for autonomous critical thought in order to support and contribute to the development of a just and civilized society.[13] This kind of dialogical consensus ought to grow out of deliberation in order for it to be effective in learning and teaching. To situate this in ODeL caring environments is to expect to be able to come to agreement each time student and lecturer perform the co-existential exercise of seeking mutual understanding. In other words, student and lecturer have the deliberative ability to come to agreement with one another because of their communicative ability to understand one another. Therefore, their strong tendency toward consensus-formation and their weak orientation toward intelligibility both exhibit the emancipatory potential of communicative action. Regardless of its quasi-transcendental qualities, language use is ingrained in interaction pragmatics. The socio-ontological relevance of discursively motivated behaviors, which are essential to the creation of democracy, reflects the political constitution of

---

12. Bloch, *Education Beyond Crisis*, 10.
13. Gray and Collison, "Accounting Education," 797–836.

spatiotemporally contingent modes of existence, with which symbolic forms originate.

If one were to engage this view, I would say that harmony should not be a qualification for dialogue and care in ODeL environments, but rather it should reflect the autonomous treatise of knowledgeable discussion responsive to the weights that are responsible for vigorous community. The deliberative paradigm is essential to critical and dialogical theory in ODeL spaces as it enables caring to emerge through a democratic teaching and learning process that serves as its primary empirical reference point. This process is meant to create legitimacy through a procedure of opinion and will produce a formation that provides publicity and transparency for the deliberative process, inclusion and equal opportunity for participation, and a justified presumption for reasonable outcomes.

Consequently, an expansive explanation of democratic citizenship pursues enduring deliberation, so that it is able to identify the better argument between majorities and minorities after the parties have temporarily reached a compromise for the sake of progress as they learn and participate together. Habermas's perception of democratic citizenship in the education process has important implications for developing higher education institutions.[14]

4. Empowering Students Through Democratic Citizenship Education in Open Distance e-Learning

The integration of democratic citizenship education within higher ODeL contexts is increasingly recognized as essential for fostering engaged and responsible citizens. As educational institutions adapt to the demands of a globalized and digital world, the principles of democratic citizenship can guide the development of curricula that emphasize critical thinking, civic engagement, and social responsibility. This approach not only prepares students to navigate

14. Warren, "Teaching with Technology," 309.

complex societal issues, but also empowers them to participate actively in democratic processes, thereby enhancing the overall quality of education in ODeL environments. The emphasis on democratic citizenship aligns with the need for educational frameworks that promote inclusivity and equity, particularly in contexts where traditional educational structures may be less accessible.[15]

Moreover, the shift towards online and distance education necessitates innovative pedagogical strategies that incorporate democratic values. Research indicates that effective citizenship education in these contexts involves leveraging digital platforms to facilitate dialogue, collaboration, and active participation among students from diverse backgrounds. By utilizing technology to create interactive learning experiences, educators can foster a sense of community and belonging, which is crucial for developing democratic competencies. This is particularly relevant in the wake of the COVID-19 pandemic, which has highlighted the importance of global citizenship and the interconnectedness of learners across geographical boundaries.[16] Thus, integrating democratic citizenship education into open distance learning not only enriches the educational experience, but also prepares students to engage meaningfully with global challenges.

The implications of democratic citizenship education extend beyond individual learning outcomes; they also contribute to the broader goal of social cohesion and democratic resilience which is underlined by caring for students in ODeL environments. As students engage with democratic principles through their education, they are more likely to develop the skills and attitudes necessary for constructive civic participation. This is particularly important in regions where democratic institutions may be fragile or under threat. By embedding democratic citizenship into the fabric of ODeL contexts, institutions can play a pivotal role in nurturing informed and active citizens who are equipped to advocate for their rights and the rights of others. This holistic approach to education not only addresses immediate educational needs, but also

15. Bartlett and Burton, *Education Studies*, 50.
16. Helm et al., "Global Citizenship," 1–18.

contributes to the long-term stability and health of democratic societies.[17]

5. Conclusion

The Fourth Industrial Revolution, along with other external factors, has significantly impacted today's students. In response, the ODeL environment has become increasingly dynamic and uncertain, shaped nevertheless in part by lecturers' efforts to foster care and dialogue. The use of LMS platforms by transformative higher education institutions—alongside the inclusion of students through a dialogical pedagogy—presents a valuable area for exploration in ODeL contexts.

Beyond enabling differentiation, ODeL systems should cultivate an environment of critical, reflective, and compassionate engagement between students and instructors, grounded in an ethics of care. Understanding how these principles intersect—particularly in relation to students' experiences of inclusion and exclusion, and their access to and use of learning resources—can offer valuable insights for educators at developing universities. In more technologically advanced ODeL environments, lecturers are encouraged to adopt a dialogical and critical approach that actively involves students in shaping policy and practice.

17. Matthieu and Junius. "Educationally Tracked Democratic Equalizers," 1–23.

CHAPTER 5

Pedagogical Action and Social Capital to Promote Care in ODeL Environments

In a classroom setting, power can rarely be completely neutralized, but it can be mitigated so that authentic deliberation between equal participants can occur. Multiple strategies can be used to mitigate power imbalances—by remaining open to all ideas (however "random") and encouraging diverse forms of expression (normative power), by seeking to draw on students' lived experience and perspectives (authoritative power), and by making classes flexible and responsive to students (administrative power).

—Nishiyama et al.

1. INTRODUCTION

In this chapter, I examine how social and cultural capital relate to the provision of care for students in the ODeL setting, and assess how deliberative democracy as a feature of online higher education might foster care through discourse. In order to nurture an engaging relationship between lecturers and students that is based on instructional action and discussion in ODeL situations, it is necessary to examine the coding theory and how these techniques might be applied.

When social capital is overlooked, it becomes a site of political and ideological struggle, often reinforcing barriers that marginalize working-class students in educational spaces.[1] Furthermore, as societal dynamics are constructed in the student-lecturer relationship, it is often the best place to produce equality or reproduce inequality because it plays an inhibiting role.[2] This chapter explores how deliberative democracy within online higher education can foster care through sustained dialogue between students and lecturers. It focuses particularly on supporting students who are most in need within the ODeL environment. A lack of such dialogue and care in student–lecturer relationships has been identified as a persistent challenge in ODeL settings.[3] The consequences of this disconnect include hindered personal and academic development, particularly within digital learning and teaching platforms.

Lecturers need to heed the call to disrupt the status quo insofar as it may contribute to the creation of a new kind of social capital and an elaborated social code among disadvantaged students,[4] enabling them to leapfrog their historic limitations and excel academically and in their chosen careers. One of this study's findings is that the education system in South Africa is structured in such a way that it largely benefits middle-class students because lecturers do not know what to do with the social habitus of working-class or disadvantaged students.[5] This is especially true since often in ODeL environments, the elaborated code is used to bring knowledge to students. This way of teaching excludes the fact that there are students who operate using a restricted code. Automatically,

1. Szreter, "Social Capital," 573–621.

2. Pietersen et al., "Social Capital, Culture, and Codes," 157–72.

3. Van den Berg, "Context Matters," 223–36; Richards and Thompson, "Challenges and Instructor Strategies," 1260421.

4. Demir, "Role of Social Capital," 100391; Lefebvre and Thomas, "I Had to Leave," 104520.

5. Motadi, *Teachers' Social Class Background*, 9–28.

working-class students are at a disadvantage because they have to adapt to the elaborated code first before they are able to grasp the knowledge that the lecturer wants to teach them.[6] Only once the elaborated code has been mastered will students benefit from the information that is being taught to them in these ODeL spaces.

2. Cultural Capital and Student Success in Open Distance e-Learning

This is where Bourdieu's theory of social and cultural capital and Bernstein's theory of social code are highly influential in making sense of how students at developing universities journey to success in a higher-education environment.[7] Bourdieu states that success in the education system is facilitated by having cultural capital and middle-class habitus.[8] This is often possessed by lecturers and middle-class students, whereas lower- or working-class students may experience higher failure rates if their social and cultural capital is not acknowledged. Bourdieu defines social capital in the following way: institutionalized networks like a family, class, or political party; [an] individual's social capital may also include networks that are bound together solely by the material or cultural transactions among its members.[9]

In conjunction with this individual or group's social frame, Bernstein similarly highlights how the student-lecturer relationship is framed. He points out the unequal distribution within higher-education systems and how they can contribute to social inequality. According to Bernstein,[10] pedagogy is a continuous process in which one or more individuals learn new behaviors,

6. White and Lowenthal, "Minority College Students," 283–318; Ballantine et al., *Sociology of Education*, 400–15.

7. Sullivan, "Bourdieu and Education," 144–66; Edgerton and Roberts, "Cultural Capital or Habitus," 193–220.

8. Ribeiro et al., "Mediating Role of Student Engagement," 2669; Burger, "Human Agency in Educational Trajectories," 952–71.

9. Bourdieu, *Forms of Capital*, 243; Fine, *Theories of Social Capital*, 36.

10. Bernstein, Pedagogy, *Symbolic Control and Identity*, 25.

knowledge, practices, and criteria from another person or from something that is considered suitable for the learner and the evaluator. This can be done from the acquirer's perspective, from the perspective of another body or bodies, or from both.[11]

The theories of Bernstein and Bourdieu will first be considered. They will be used to problematize how online learning and teaching only benefits some students and not others.[12] In both face-to-face and online instruction, lecturers predominantly use the "social code" and "social capital" to engage with their students, which in the words of Bernstein[13] can be said to be an unequal distribution of quality education. It could be argued that if online learning was properly integrated in a way that acknowledged students' existing social and cultural capital,[14] this could in turn contribute to positive outcomes and enhance students' performance.[15] To illustrate this further, one can draw connections between the recognition of students' capital and the formation of care-based relationships.

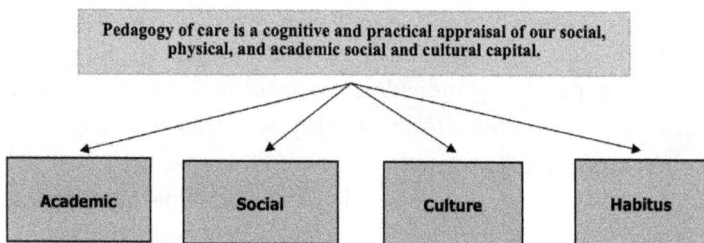

| Pedagogy of care is a cognitive and practical appraisal of our social, physical, and academic social and cultural capital. |

| Academic | Social | Culture | Habitus |

Figure 3. Social Capital and Pedagogical Action to Encourage Care in OdeL Settings

Students' social, cultural, and habitual capital are evaluated both cognitively and practically as part of the pedagogy of care, which acknowledges how these elements influence their needs and

11. Gabel, "Problems with Critical Pedagogy," 177–201.
12. Basar et al., "Challenges of Online Learning," 119–29.
13. Bernstein, "Language and Social Class," 271–76.
14. Lamont and Lareau, "Cultural Capital," 153–68.
15. De Clercq, "Educational Inequalities," 1–22.

learning experiences. Lecturers in ODeL, for instance, can employ group projects that represent the cultural backgrounds of their students, creating a feeling of community and building social capital through peer interactions.[16] Furthermore, by addressing personal struggles and utilizing local expertise, mentorship programs that link students to community resources can foster compassion and enhance the educational experience in ODeL settings.[17]

I would argue that the concepts of social capital and social code are intertwined within ODeL environments and can be powerful constructs in creating positive teaching relationships, which would result in greater upward mobility for students at developing universities. An example of how social capital and code could be used to enable democracy is students sharing information in class based on their own identity and lecturers using online platforms to support struggling students.[18] In other words, social capital and code, if acknowledged by middle-class lecturers who mainly teach working-class students, would result in success for students as they progress in life and could result in even further social upliftment and equality.[19]

3. Socioeconomic Challenges in Open Distance e-Learning

According to Samuelsson and Bøyum,[20] deliberative democracy in education can be defined as a reaction to some of the issues that modern democracies and democratic ideas are confronting. The questions raised in evaluating how deliberative democracy involved in online higher education can inspire care through dialogue is underscored by the sociological theories of Bourdieu and

16. Venter, "Student Online Collaborations," 335–53.

17. Olivier et al., *Contextualised Open Educational Practices*, 203–16.

18. Salimi, "Online Social Capital," 6599–620.

19. Pitsoe and Letseka, "Social Capital and Open Distance e-Learning," 202–12; Nguyen, "Low-income Students," 497.

20. Samuelsson and Bøyum, "Education for Deliberative Democracy," 75–94.

Bernstein. The work of these scholars helps to critically analyze how online learning and teaching platforms are adding to or detracting from the student-lecturer relationship, which does not preclude socioeconomic challenges. This chapter will outline precisely how the aforementioned conceptual framework of social capital and code speaks to ontology, truth, and method as it relates to the power relations that either consciously or unconsciously exist between student and lecturer.[21]

The Bourdieusian and Bernsteinian concepts of social capital and code produce a language that aims to either promote or limit educational advancement in higher education spaces. It should be mentioned that because cultural differences are often exacerbated in South Africa, the language used on online learning and teaching platforms can either improve or worsen communication.[22] Many academics believe that social capital is located in the relationships that people have with one another, rather than in any one individual.[23] This illustrates the widening gap between working-class students and middle-class lecturers and should be especially noted in ODeL settings.

Every social context inherently shapes its own unique language, which in turn influences the mechanisms of social control within that environment.[24] This social control manifests as a set of norms and expectations that are imposed on individuals' habitus –essentially their dispositions, behaviors, and perceptions. In educational settings, particularly in open-distance environments, this social control is crucial as it dictates how knowledge is constructed, shared, and resisted.[25] As students engage with the educational material, their understanding and interpretation are colored by the specific language and social dynamics of their context, which can either facilitate or hinder their learning experiences.

21. Niati, "Bourdieu's Habitus," 1–14.

22. Halpern, *Social Capital*, 142–44.

23. Lin, *Theory of Social Structure*, 5–14; Lorenzen, "Social Capital and Localised Learning," 799–817.

24. Brown, *Vulnerability and Young People*, 16–8.

25. Giroux, *Theory and Resistance in Education*, 10–5.

Furthermore, the relationship between social capital and advancement in higher education spaces plays a significant role in delineating the dynamics between dominating and dominated classes. In educational frameworks, particularly those that are open and distance-oriented, the language used not only reflects but also reinforces existing power structures.[26] For instance, students from marginalized backgrounds may struggle to access the dominant forms of knowledge and social capital embedded in educational materials, which can hinder their advancement in higher ODeL education. This situation can lead to a misalignment between their habitus and the expectations of the educational system, prompting a critical need for educators to be aware of these disparities.[27] By recognizing and addressing the specific social contexts of their students, educators can foster a more inclusive and equitable learning environment.

4. Enhancing Care Through Dialogue in Learning in Open Distance e-Learning

The contextualization of language within education is pivotal for guiding habitus and shaping students' experiences in open-distance learning spaces.[28] When educators are attuned to the social contexts that influence their students, they can better support their development and promote resilience against social control mechanisms. This requires not only adapting pedagogical approaches to be more inclusive, but also fostering critical engagement with the material in ODeL spaces, rather than merely repeating content that fails to reflect the evolving realities of contemporary communities.[29] By nurturing an environment that values diverse perspectives, social capital and advancement, lecturers can empower students to navigate and challenge the social controls imposed on

26. Daniels and Greguras, *Why Deliberative Democracy,* 1202–29.

27. Burke, "Capitals and Habitus", 65–82

28. De Moll et al., "Students' Academic Habitus," 190–220.

29. Walton and Engelbrecht, "Inclusive Education," 2138–56.

them, thereby enhancing their educational outcomes and fostering a sense of agency in their ODeL learning journey.[30]

Bourdieu's way of looking at habitus is to interrogate the education system as a process of cultural and social reproduction. Bourdieu's work was influenced by Karl Marx, widely regarded as the intellectual founder of conflict theory, particularly in relation to higher education within the sociology of education.[31] Bourdieu focused on the concepts of cultural capital and symbolic violence. He saw symbolic violence as power that enforces certain meanings on people.[32] This is seen as a legitimate way of hiding the power relations that might be overlooked by institutions of higher learning. This power relation is also found in the education system, as education benefits the middle class because of the middle class's symbolic representation.[33] The representations of cultural dominance consist of many factors, such as language, ideas, and the knowledge of music, art, and literature.

The intricate system of differentiations that influences how individuals act upon each another can be understood through various lenses, including legal, economic, cultural, and social. In educational contexts, particularly in ODeL environments, these differentiations are critical as they shape the experience of students from diverse backgrounds.[34] For instance, legal frameworks and traditions of status and privilege can create barriers to access and success in education. Students from marginalized communities may face systemic challenges in the ODeL eco-systems that limit their ability to fully engage with the learning process, thereby perpetuating existing inequalities.[35] Understanding these differentiations is essential for educators who aim to create equitable learning experiences that account for the varied backgrounds and resources of their students.

30. Bozkurt et al., "Openness in Education," 76–112.
31. Sadovnik et al., "Exploring Education," 2000.
32. Carter Andrews et al., "Call to Action," 205–8.
33. Brantlinger, *Dividing Classes*, 40.
34. Brevik, "Student Teachers' Practice," 34–45.
35. Daniels et al., "Academics' Experiences of Precarity," 40–62.

Moreover, the objectives pursued by those in positions of power within educational systems often reflect broader societal goals, such as the maintenance of privileges or the accumulation of profit. In ODeL settings, this can manifest in the commercialization of education, where profit motives may overshadow the educational needs of students.[36] Educators and institutions may prioritize metrics of success that align with financial gain, potentially sidelining the holistic development of students. Additionally, the exercise of power in educational settings can occur through various means—whether through authoritative mandates, economic inequalities, or cultural capital. These power dynamics play a vital role in shaping students' experiences and outcomes, emphasizing the necessity for educators to critically reflect on how these forces impact their pedagogical practices in ODeL eco-systems.[37]

The forms and degrees of institutionalization within ODeL environments further complicate the landscape of power relations. Educational institutions may blend traditional practices with contemporary legal structures and evolving customs, resulting in varied levels of effectiveness in addressing students' needs.[38] The degree to which these institutions operationalize power relations can range from explicit regulations to more nuanced, informal practices that influence student interactions and learning opportunities. This complexity highlights the importance of fostering an inclusive culture in ODeL that not only recognizes, but actively works to dismantle the barriers created by these differentiations. By doing so, lecturers can better support the diverse needs of students in ODeL settings,[39] promoting an environment where all learners can thrive and engage meaningfully with the educational process.

These factors play an integral role in the education system, as well as the working environment of social classes. According

36. Sincer, "Teaching Diversity," 183–92.

37. Shi and Sercombe, "Poverty and Inequality," 1–28.

38. Smith, *Diversity's Promise*, 200.

39. Doyle, *Facilitating Learning*, 26.

to Hillier and Rooksby,[40] to have a sense of these social capital and code stratification factors, participants need to understand and "play the game" in the following way: all participants must be continuously aware of and receptive to the game. It necessitates evaluating the resources, strengths, and vulnerabilities of both the opponents and one's own teammates. Improvisation, adaptability, and most importantly, the ability to predict the actions of one's opponents and teammates are necessary in ODeL contexts.

The concept of cultural capital can be used to explain how the education system in South Africa forms part of a socialization of reproduction.[41] This means that the education system perpetuates the same working-class and middle-class citizens as it always has. Any education system, including those in developing universities, has the potential to socialize students into reproducing educational inequalities, channeling working-class students into working-class jobs and middle-class students into middle-class roles.[42]

5. Intersection of Language and Agency in Open Distance e-Learning

If one considers online learning and teaching platforms, such as Moodle and Blackboard, from a philosophical framework, one may end up with what Bernstein[43] called social language that can be internalized, incorporated, objectified, or institutionalized. Put differently, when social capital is overlooked, it becomes a site of political and ideological struggle—often reinforcing structures that disadvantage black students in educational spaces. Furthermore, as societal dynamics are constructed in the student-lecturer relationship, it is often the best place to produce or reproduce inequality because it plays an inhibiting role. The theoretical framework of this chapter positions the online learning and teaching

40. Hillier and Rooksby, "In Habitus," 23.

41. Fataar, "Pedagogical Justice," 52–75; Cross and Atinde, "Pedagogy of the Marginalized," 308–25; Ndlovu, "Pedagogic Domain," 205–24.

42. Calarco, *Negotiating Opportunities*, 12.

43. Bernstein, *Class, Codes and Control*, 20.

space within both a Bourdieusian (social capital) and Bernsteinian (social code) perspective, as both theorists highlight how the dominant class—often represented by lecturers—consciously or unconsciously overlooks students' social and cultural capital and communicative codes. This in turn inhibits students' development and growth—it is the asset of the bourgeoisie/capitalist.[44] However, every social class comes into the education system possessing a cultural capital, consisting of their own knowledge of music, art, and literature, all of which plays an important part in the education of students. The way this presents itself in online higher education platforms is in the form of curricular, pedagogical, and pupil evaluation practices.

In the context of ODeL platforms, the digital divide in many African countries, including South Africa, exacerbates existing inequalities.[45] For instance, students from underprivileged backgrounds often lack access to reliable internet and technology, which hinders their ability to engage fully with these platforms.[46] This digital divide not only affects their learning outcomes, but also reinforces societal hierarchies, as those with greater resources are better positioned to benefit from online education. Student-lecturer relationships on ODeL platforms plays a crucial role in either challenging or perpetuating inequality.[47] As societal dynamics are constructed in these interactions, the potential for educational spaces to reproduce existing power structures becomes evident.

The historical legacy of apartheid still affects educational procedures in South Africa where children from marginalized backgrounds may encounter racial prejudice or a lack of support from instructors, further impeding their educational opportunities.[48] This situation is a prime example of how social capital may be used as an ideological and political instrument to limit working-class

44. Moore, *Thinker and the Field*, 150.

45. Gasa, "Digital Divide," 562–7.

46. Zongozzi and Ngubane, "Equitable Access," 1525.

47. Mtombeni, *Use of Technology*, 7–8; Mtombeni, *Use of Technology*, 9–10.

48. Chiramba and Ndofirepi, "Access and Success in Higher Education," 56–75.

children's potential when it is disregarded.[49] ODeL platforms have the potential of becoming places of exclusion rather than empowerment if these disparities are not addressed, which would eventually prolong the cycle of disadvantage in African higher educational institutions.[50] The structure of online learning environments and how to make them more inclusive and equitable for all students must be critically reevaluated in order to address these issues.

6. CONCLUSION

This chapter explored the potential of online higher education to foster meaningful dialogue and compassion between lecturers and students by examining how deliberative democracy functions within ODeL environments through the lens of the caring principle. It also analyzed the relevance of social capital and social code models within the sociological framework of care. The discussion highlighted the ways in which socioeconomic factors in online learning contexts at emerging universities intersect with the procedural challenges of caring pedagogy and ideology. Ultimately, this analysis underscores the idea that education, including higher education, often unfortunately acts as a process that reinforces social divisions by categorizing individuals into distinct groups based on their circumstances, rather than bridging social divides.

---

49. Tzanakis, "Social Capital in Bourdieu's Theory," 2–23; Rogoš[set breve over s]ić and Baranović, "Social Capital and Educational Achievements," 81–100.

50. Kgari-Masondo and Chimbunde, "Progress of an African Student," 323–39.

CHAPTER 6

Embracing Student Voice and Prioritizing Engaged Pedagogy to Foster Care in ODeL Environments

Engaged pedagogy highlights the importance of independent thinking and each student finding his or her unique voice; this recognition is usually empowering for students. This is especially important for students who otherwise may not have felt that they were "worthy", that they had anything of value to contribute.

—bell hooks

1. INTRODUCTION

The current design of South Africa's educational system favors pupils from the middle to upper classes, many of whom are white. The impoverished and vulnerable working class, many of whom are black, make up the majority of South Africa's population. The pattern of favoring the upper and middle classes over the working class will continue if children enrolled in universities that go through the same social reproduction process. While this is certainly feasible in any university, it might be simpler in ODeL settings because to the lack of face-to-face interactions.

Due to their background, past educational experiences, and incapacity to successfully adjust to the educational system, working-class students are at a clear disadvantage when they first enter the South African education system.[1] Due to the way they were socialized at home, middle-class students come to school with prior knowledge, which facilitates their adjustment to the educational setting because they already understand the procedure, how it operates, and what is expected of them. The middle-class student is raised in a setting where academic success is expected of them. They receive instruction in reading, writing, and interpreting their surroundings—fundamental abilities that benefit them at school.

2. EQUITABLE LEARNING OPPORTUNITIES FOR ALL STUDENTS IN OPEN DISTANCE E-LEARNING

Lecturers should use Bourdieu's theory as a guide to address the issues in our education system. It ought to help instructors understand that not every student has the same amount of cultural capital and expertise when they first enroll at university. Both middle-class and working-class students should have their past knowledge assessed by their lecturers, who should then expand on it. According to Hailikari et al.,[2] lecturers shouldn't presume that every student has the same amount of prior knowledge. In order for working-class pupils to attain the same level of academic achievement as their middle-class counterparts, they should strive to expedite learning.

As Venter[3] argues, learning can occur in a variety of settings, including ODeL environments, and people learn for a variety of reasons throughout their lives. The entire learning process includes more than just formal education. The entire learning process includes more than just formal education. As students move between and within various learning platforms, the concept of a

1. Spaull, "Poverty and Privilege," 436–47.
2. Hailikari, "Relevance of Prior Knowledge," 113.
3. Venter, "Student Online Collaborations," 335–53.

personal learning environment (PLE) has emerged as an inclusive and collaborative space. Such environments ultimately promote the inclusion of student voices, fostering a sense of care, particularly in contexts where it is most needed.

The elaborated code and the confined code are two sub-concepts of the code theory. Those that care about coding theory should, as a result, embrace their students' opinions. This is also applicable to the ODeL environment. According to Bernstein, the middle class uses the elaborated code, while the working class uses the restricted code, in part due to linguistic differences as English is the lingua franca in South Africa, but it is not the first language of the majority of the population. People's basic assumptions are shaped by restricted code, often without critical reflection on underlying biases.[4] This can conflict with the notion of shared identities and interests, or with a cultural identity that lessens the need to articulate intentions explicitly through language. Such dynamics must be considered when developing caring pedagogies.

Although a close relationship necessitates a complex code, getting to know someone well implies that you share identities, interests, and expectations, though this does not always mean that you agree.[5] These codes are a means of using language to explain the differences in class. Bernstein questions why middle-class students do better than working-class ones in the context of his native United Kingdom. This is particularly valid in ODeL settings in South Africa. For this reason, I have decided to use this theory to assess how ODeL's deliberative democracy might encourage care through engagement and dialogue.

3. Understanding the Social Habitus in Open Distance e-Learning Spaces

The higher education system in South Africa, including developing universities, is structured in such a way that it largely benefits

4. Obiukwu, "Influence of Socioeconomic Background," 15.
5. Ivinson, "Bernstein's Restricted Codes," 539–54.

middle-class students because lecturers do not know what to do with the social habitus of working-class students.[6] For disadvantaged, mainly black students, technology represents more than just digital connectivity, as well as physical hardware and software; it is also associated with difficulty with the application and assignment submission processes and resource accessibility. What is more, most South African higher education institutions make use of the elaborated code: lecturers assume all students are able to perform well on online platforms as they share knowledge with students from varied socioeconomic strata. This way of teaching excludes the fact that there are students who do not have access to the same resources and are unable to engage online the way that other students do. These students really need to embraced and prioritized. Automatically, the working-class, black student is at a disadvantage because they have to adapt to the elaborated code first before they are able to grasp the knowledge that the lecturer wants to teach them[7] and they need to use technology that they may not always be able to access.

Only once the elaborated code has been mastered will students benefit from the information that is being taught to them.[8] Any learning and teaching platform reflects the presence of socially conscious and educated individuals. In pursuit of this broader educational aim, Waghid et al.[9] argue that South African universities are being challenged by the Department of Education to reshape their pedagogical approaches in response to the demands of the Fourth Industrial Revolution, with the hope that such efforts will contribute to economic prosperity, job creation, and the empowerment of marginalized communities.

In order for faculties at developing universities to uplift marginalized communities, we have to elaborate on the code that students use. Indeed, much analysis is needed, so that generalizations, ungrounded social capital arguments and higher-level

6. Yee, "Rules of Engagement," 831–58.

7. Arnot and Reay, *Pedagogic Voices*, 30–40.

8. Stahl, *Narratives of Reconstruction*, 21–30.

9. Waghid, "Advancing Cosmopolitan Education," 4.

concepts are not superficially considered. According to Skerrit,[10] middle-class students have no problem performing well in school and in online higher education because they have an elaborated code. The transmission of knowledge is easy because they know how to analyze information and make generalizations: they have the ability to develop constructive arguments. These abilities give middle-class students an advantage over working-class students and also explain why middle-class students perform better in higher education online learning platforms than their working-class counterparts. Fataar[11] posits that power marginalization should be viewed as a fluid process in terms of how students determine feasible educational options, rather than as indicating a standstill linked to material poverty or necessarily implying a lack of aspirational commitment.

Differences exist between education systems that serve the working class and those that serve the middle class.[12] They differ in terms of the curricula and teaching methods used by teachers at school level, so that it may lead to easy access for middle-class students to higher education spaces. These differences result in educational inequality among social classes.[13]

4. Rethinking Educational Stratification in Open Distance e-Learning Spaces

Based on my personal experience as a lecturer, I have noted that middle-class students perform better academically than working-class students. The restricted code and the elaborated code that separates the social classes are two examples of the linguistic tools which results in disparities in academic achievement among students from different backgrounds. Bernstein claimed that

10. Skerritt, "Code for Success," 274–276.

11. Fataar, "Terms of (Mis)recognition," 7.

12. Bhana, "Race Matters," 355.

13. Abbas and McLean, "Tackling Inequality," 244.

working-class language was lacking, which caused his detractors to call his code theory a deficit theory.

From a South African standpoint, students' English language skills have a significant impact on the social code in online higher education, regardless of how elaborate or restrictive it is. This is especially evident in ODeL contexts, where several marking schemes and procedures are used. The limited code is typically used by students who speak English as a second or third language. Anecdotally, this is frequently the reason why African students from other countries perform better than their black South African counterparts: in other words, their access to the complex academic code is made possible by their apparently superior command of English.

Bourdieu faced criticism for the way he conceptualized the link between teaching and learning, just as Bernstein did. Bourdieu's theory is entirely closed. It is utterly negative and cynical. We are destined to be stratified forever in it. We are stuck in our skins. Only inside an iron circle can we switch places. If that is the case, will the middle class be the only ones who gain from our education system in the long run? In an effort to embrace student voices and prioritize engaged pedagogy that fosters care in ODeL environments, Bourdieu's theory falls short in recognizing how power relations actively shape teaching and learning dynamics. Consequently, both organizational and social stratification are reshaped and restructured.[14]

5. Fostering Student-Lecturer Engagement in Open Distance e-Learning Spaces

We can aspire to a constructive online pedagogy[15] in which students are taught by lecturers who demonstrate a strong cognitive presence, while also fostering connection among diverse socially embodied groups, provided that social stratification is acknowledged rather than overlooked. In other words, a good online

14. Sadovnik, "Bernstein's Theory," 48–63.
15. Cole, *Education, Equality*, 2013.

learning environment is one that allows for the use of effective teaching techniques, thereby enhancing students' online learning experiences.[16] This calls for more funding for online education by giving instructors the chance to participate in professional development training pertaining to online learning. This will allow them to learn different methods of teaching online and satisfy the diverse needs of students.

It became clear during COVID-19 that university lecturers' professional development was rarely given priority, highlighting the difficulty that ODeL settings are presented with. This lack of professional development limits the potential for high-quality education to occur and makes it extremely difficult for students and lecturers to interact, communicate, and care for one another on these platforms.[17] It is recommended that universities, including ODeL universities, make a greater investment in the training of their lecturers, so that they can fulfil the diverse needs of their students and are familiar with the online teaching modalities that ought to lead to engaged and caring pedagogies.

6. CONCLUSION

In the South African context, it is largely the middle class, many of whom are white, that benefits from the reproductive nature of the current system. One overlooked yet critical aspect of ODeL education is its tendency to exclude working-class, black students from advancing academically through structural mechanisms, such as biased evaluation or high failure rates. This exclusion functions as a form of academic gatekeeping. Meaningful transformation in higher education cannot occur unless this socioeconomic inequality is openly acknowledged and actively addressed. At the intersection of these urgent issues, we need a perspective that illuminates, rather than obscures the realities of power and access. This is where hope resides. Much like an MRI, COVID-19 has revealed

---

16. Waghid, "Teaching and Learning," 225-28.
17. Phejane, "The New Normal," 164–78.

the deep structural inequalities in South Africa—our society's "social bones". To help disadvantaged students transcend historical limitations and thrive, particularly in ODeL environments, lecturers must be willing to challenge entrenched norms and foster new forms of social capital and more inclusive discursive codes.

CHAPTER 7

Pedagogy of Care and the Future for Developing ODeL Universities

Studies have shown that teacher care makes transformative and positive impacts upon university students' learning and behaviors, including increased academic motivation, engagement, resilience, and success.

—Anne Tang, Caroline Walker-Gleaves, and Julie Rattray

1. INTRODUCTION

The optimal use of online or hybrid teaching platforms is critical to ensuring that higher education environments in developing universities should not be left behind in the Fourth Industrial Revolution (4IR). Several technological platforms that were embraced during the COVID-19 lockdown have the potential to increase students' digital access, but have simultaneously overwhelmed teachers and students. It seems ironic, therefore, that the very technology that enables online teaching and learning to take place in higher education is often the same factor that inhibits student success and limits teachers in their pedagogy. Regardless of format, the teaching and learning encounter should not come at the expense of caring for the actual student in the ever-changing hybrid teaching model that most tertiary institutions have since adopted. Therefore, my interest is on how care pedagogies might improve online teaching and learning at developing universities.

This chapter not only surveys various perspectives, but also contributes to the ongoing effort to frame caring pedagogies within online teaching and learning environments. It highlights the importance of social presence and student-centered learning, drawing on Freire's pedagogical philosophy to foreground the value of care in teaching and learning relationships within an ever-evolving higher education landscape. This also suggests that a pedagogy of care is central to the future development of ODeL universities, as it emphasizes the potential for meaningful interaction between lecturers and students, fostering critical thinking, inclusive learning environments, and genuine participation. Additionally, these theories foreground the use of care pedagogies to establish encouraging, nurturing, and transformational online learning environments. The chapter contends that the responsibility to offer an online democratic space of care is limited and is largely the role of university teachers as representatives of the institution. It should be reflected not only by the number of students engaged in class content, but also by the embodied cultural capital that students bring to ODeL learning spaces.

2. Quality Interactions Between Lecturers and Students in Open Distance e-Learning Spaces

It is not surprising that we find ourselves working in an educational context where addressing deep-rooted inequalities is essential to the foundation of pedagogies of care, particularly if we hope to transform a society in which severe socioeconomic disparities not only persist but are, in some cases, actively reinforced within educational spaces. COVID-19 has only increased this fact. This is highlighted by a recent study done by Badaru and Adu, *Platformisation of Education: An Analysis of South African Universities' Learning Management Systems* in the following way:

In the midst of the pandemic, South Africa's 2020/2021 academic year got underway, and educational institutions faced the pressing need to enhance their online course navigation and curriculum, administer online tests, expand student participation in remote learning, and fortify their ability to use ICT in emergency situations.[1]

The growing crisis in online teaching and learning has highlighted critical questions about the quality of engagement between university lecturers and students. It has also drawn attention to the extent to which such engagement can foster a positive and caring learning environment—whether that reality is viewed as complex or straightforward.[2] This chapter responds to the need to frame pedagogies of care within blended and online learning environments, particularly to address the quality and impact of lecturer–student interactions—relationships that are often neglected in digital contexts.[3] This is especially important in the wake of the pandemic, as it is vital to confront and redress the inequalities that continue to shape educational experiences in its aftermath.[4]

Given that online higher education teaching and learning are mainly "faceless",[5] this chapter contends that the responsibility to offer an online democratic space of care is limited and is largely left at the door of the lecturer, instead of being institutionalized. The question may be asked whether this responsibility is adequately discharged by the parties involved and to what extent this plays out in online educational spaces. In raising such questions, social class inevitably comes into focus, particularly given its significant influence on online teaching and learning.[6] Yet, social class is rarely considered in student engagement strategies, with many university lecturers primarily focused on meeting course

1. Badaru and Adu, "Platformisation of Education," 67.
2. La Fleur and Dlamini, "Learner-centric Pedagogies," 4–20.
3. Lucas and Vicente, "Double-edged Sword," 1–21.
4. Neuwirth et al., "Reimagining Higher Education," 141–156.
5. Fouche and Andrews, "Student Feedback during COVID-19," 133–55.
6. Czerniewicz, "Wake-up Call," 946–67.

or module outcomes.[7] Students' beliefs, however, are shaped not only by their individual experiences in online environments, but also by their social interactions and their interpretations of formal, research-based knowledge, especially as they engage with digital technologies such as learning management systems.

3. Understanding the Liminal Space of Open Distance e-Learning Spaces

Noddings[8] argues that in this kind of socially connected awareness on online higher education platforms, it is difficult to "proximate ... under whose gaze I fall" unless there is a deliberate effort to foster interaction and engagement. This includes university lecturers being able to navigate online teaching and learning platforms, and not simply setting up digital strategies to support students' needs in the 4IR to only "tick the box".[9] This might have to happen in a stop-and-start manner because continued evaluation needs to be taken into consideration for students and lecturers to grow and develop in the teaching and learning process. However, social awareness with students might be difficult to foster and end up being a burden for the lecturer for the very same reason that the 4IR has necessitated this digital transformation in terms of flexible online teaching and learning at developing universities.[10]

Max Weber[11] places this kind of transformation on the ontological locality of caring: it is a liminal space that has ethical implications. This raises related issues of wealth, power, and status—not as problems in themselves, but as factors that create a mismatch between lecturer and student on online platforms, where it is often assumed that both parties engage with technology equally.[12]

---

7. Mpungose and Khoza, "Postgraduate Student Experiences," 1–16.
8. Noddings, "Feminine Approach to Ethics," 113.
9. Naidoo, "Postgraduate Mathematics Education," 568.
10. Zawacki-Richter et al., "Research on AI Applications," 27.
11. Weber, *Methodology of Social Sciences*, 60.
12. Chirinda et al., "Teaching Mathematics," 177.

It is, therefore, crucial that it is never assumed that just because teaching and learning is taking place on online higher education platforms, care that is impactful and helps the helpless is also taking place. This is what this research problematizes and there is real apprehension for opponents to this idea for various reasons. For example, Selwyn surmises that "as with digital technologies in general, digital data do not offer a neat technical fix to education dilemmas—no matter how compelling the output might be".[13]

In analyzing access to data and technology in a country like South Africa, one needs to consider the large gaps between the "haves" and "have-nots" in a society.[14] One might even go so far as separating people into working (proletariat), middle (bourgeoisie), and upper class to understand these difficult, but real complexities. Separation and differences cause much conflict to arise, with the poor fighting for equality for all, and the rich fighting to maintain their prestigious position within society as technology advances.[15] This creates an unequal dynamic between the 4IR, students, university lecturers, and online teaching and learning, invoking the perspectives of the founding figures of sociological conflict theory.[16] Put differently, the relationship between the lecturer and the student should be considered through the lens of caring for the individual student holistically in the online space. However difficult it may seem to the lecturer, the definition of caring for students and its associated moral competence is making sure the needs of the person being cared for are satisfied.[17]

13. Selwyn, "Is Technology Good?," 16.
14. Makumbe, "E-learning," 621–41.
15. Johnstone, *Class, Race, and Gold*, 110.
16. Gredley, *Socially Just Pedagogies*, 35–38.
17. Feldman, "Ethics of Care," 1–17.

4. FEEDBACK AS A MARKER OF STUDENT MOTIVATION IN OPEN DISTANCE e-LEARNING

Because of the social presence on digital university platforms, lecturers ought to see the importance of human relationships in online learning. This is where establishing a social presence through dialogue is essential for creating a sense of connection and engagement among students in the learning process.[18] What results is a caring pedagogical approach that supports student development by encouraging a sense of belonging,[19] empathy, and trust between students and lecturers.[20]

The social presence of lecturers in online higher education is crucial for bridging this gap and creating lasting connections.[21] In online learning environments, a strong teacher social presence creates a sense of connection and fosters a welcoming environment.[22] Lecturers may overcome the distance between them and their students by actively participating in discussions, giving quick feedback, and encouraging a feeling of community. This will help to develop a climate where students feel valued and involved. Students who feel like their presence and contributions count in the online classroom are more motivated to learn.[23]

5. TRANSFORMING OPEN DISTANCE e-LEARNING THROUGH A STUDENT-CENTERED APPROACH

In human connections, trust and rapport are essential; this is also true in the online classroom. By showcasing their knowledge, being approachable, and genuinely caring about their students'

---

18. Hossain et al., "Role of Social Media," 4–12.

19. Tate and Warschauer, "Equity in Online Learning," 192–206.

20. Tackie, "Establishing Social Presence," 23328584211069525; Greenhow, "Diverse Perspectives," 1842–46.

21. Händel et al., "Synchronous Online Learning," 10405–28.

22. Munoz et al., "Enhancing Online Learning," 339–57.

23. Alger and Eyckmans, "Positive Surprises," 53–84.

well-being, teachers can establish trust through their social presence.[24] Teachers can build meaningful connections with their students by fostering an environment where they feel free to express their ideas, ask questions, and share their struggles.[25] This increases student happiness and a sense of belonging.

In relation to student-centered learning, developing universities are uniquely positioned to foster transformative, socially just environments in which online technological spaces are grounded in dialogue and caring pedagogies.[26] It is evident that this perspective speaks to student-centered learning where student empowerment is the main focus as it enables university teachers and students to promote discussion and care.[27] Student agency is facilitated by dialogue, which gives students a say in how their educational experiences are shaped.[28]

With student-centered learning, the focus is on the learner throughout the educational process. Through this, online higher education platforms can empower students to take control of their learning process by promoting active interaction.[29] Lecturers have a key role to play in creating this kind of climate that appreciates students' views, perspectives, and contributions. Students have the chance to communicate with lecturers and peers through online conversations, virtual group projects, and interactive learning activities, building real human relationships that improve results and general pleasure in the learning experience.[30]

24. Payne et al., "Under-served Students," 1–18; Stone, "Margins to Mainstream," 139–49.

25. Northcote, "Reframing Contemporary Online Education," 1–32; Lemoine et al., "Online Learning," 28–44.

26. Toh, "Sustainable Pedagogical Reform," 145–69; Weisberger, "Social Roles of Teachers," 103344.

27. Krikowa, *Reflexive Transformative Approach*, 68–99; Pownall, "Academic Identity," 1–15.

28. Scanlon and Connolly, "Teacher Agency," 104291; Bough and Sainz, "Digital Learning Experiences," 375–93; Barrot and Fernando, "Mediating Role of Teachers," 1–23.

29. Attard et al., *Student-Centered Learning*, 29–36.

30. Dixon et al., *Online Student-centred Discussion*, 256–262.

Another consequence of student-centered learning is collaborative learning. This is where students are given the chance to collaborate with lecturers, who promote idea sharing, group problem-solving, and mutual learning.[31] Students are able to have thoughtful conversations, give criticism, and encourage one anothers' development through the use of online forums and communication tools. By fostering a feeling of community and shared learning, these collaborative events build the bonds between lecturers and students, as well as within the student body.[32]

6. Conclusion

In any ODeL setting, the approach of student-centered learning recognizes the importance of students' total growth and welfare. Lecturers prioritize their students' social, emotional, and mental well-being in addition to their academic progress. By promoting candid conversations, offering guidance, and demonstrating empathy and understanding, lecturers build strong relationships with their audience. For students, this establishes a network of support that promotes resilience, success, and general well-being. Ultimately, dialogue and care pedagogies, grounded in the perspectives outlined above, ensure that students are not only participants in the ODeL learning environment, but active partners in shaping teaching and learning around their individual and collective needs, aspirations, and potential.

31. Buchanan, "Improving the Quality of Teaching," 345–56; Choo et al., "Patterns of Interaction," 307–14.

32. Hussin, "Online Interaction," 4–12.

CHAPTER 8

A Transformative Caring Approach in Teaching and Learning in ODeL Spaces

As scholars and students, we no longer simply learn to internalize, monitor, and manage our own alienation inside, but work explicitly outside. Thus, we aim to collectively engage in a process of critical questioning, motivating us to reconsider our pedagogical practices, resisting, and dismantling dominant structures as a means to reconceptualize higher education.

—Karla Boluk and Sandro Carnicelli

1. INTRODUCTION

The main research question of this chapter relates to how a deliberative democracy can lead to pedagogies of dialogue and care in higher education online spaces. To answer that question, this chapter makes the case that lecturers should be informed by the principles of social presence and student-centered learning as key perspectives in ODeL environments. These theoretical foundations will be explored as a means of understanding how teaching and learning relationships between lecturers and students in developing higher education institutions can be improved.

2. Reflection and Action as a Transformative Approach in Open Distance e-Learning

This chapter adopts an open form of critical enquiry inspired by Freire,[1] exploring the extent to which university teachers are willing or unwilling to engage with advances in online teaching and learning technologies. This engagement is examined through the lens of a care pedagogy, not merely because of its complexity, but because it is essential for meaningful human interaction.[2] This is described by Freire, noting that "reflection and action in close interaction are the necessary conditions for dialogical action, and if one of them is prevented, the word becomes an empty word, one that cannot denounce the world, for denunciation is impossible without commitment to transform, and there is no transformation without action".[3] University teachers and students possess a certain belief about the teaching and learning space that is not always experienced in the same way. For example, issues with the type of online teaching and learning platform can be tricky because they often can be tools of opportunity or create further hurdles for students wanting to advance.[4]

If online higher education is constructed around the lecturer and student relationship (social consciousness) and not just technology,[5] then the value proposition for a pedagogy of care as a holistic pedagogy will lead students towards active democracy.[6] To this end, the consequential implications for value-added education in a caring 4IR context are built on theoretical values and ideologies that consider evidence and consequences of what students and university teachers bring as beings the learning process.[7]

---

1. Freire, *Pedagogy of the Oppressed*, 13.
2. Stephens et al., "Social-class Disparities," 67–73.
3. Freire, *Pedagogy of the Oppressed*, 87.
4. Dias et al., "DeepLMS," 1–17; Feldman, "Ethics of Care," 1–17.
5. Elumalai et al., "Quality of e-Learning," 731–53.
6. Bosio, "Global Citizenship Education," 1–15.
7. Johnston et al., *Conceptualizing the Digital University*, 39–40.

3. Balancing Technology and Care in Open Distance e-Learning

A caring approach by lecturers in the online teaching and learning space may resonate with some, but is often overlooked by many.[8] This widespread disregard for what Feldman describes as a form of "phantom" power[9] can subtly, yet significantly, shape our decisions in online teaching and learning environments. How does this happen? Well, one of the most common complaints about online teaching and learning is the lack of empathy and understanding shown by some university teachers towards their students. The online space can be a very isolating and lonely experience for some students, especially those who are introverted or who have personal issues that make it difficult for them to connect with others. In such situations, caring university teachers can have a profound impact, offering vital support and guidance to struggling students—not only to enhance learning, but because it is a matter of social justice.[10]

Unfortunately, some university teachers do not seem to understand the importance of building a personal relationship with their students. They may focus solely on delivering their university modules without taking the time to check in with their students and find out how they are doing. This can create a feeling of detachment between students and their university teachers, leading to a breakdown in communication and a lack of motivation among students.[11] In addition, the lack of accountability in online teaching and learning can exacerbate the problem. Some university teachers may simply post lectures online and expect students to do the rest without any guidance or support.[12] This approach to teaching can be demoralizing for students, especially those who are struggling with the material. The lack of feedback and

---

8. Martin and Bolliger, "Engagement Matters," 205–22.

9. Feldman, "Ethics of Care," 1–17.

10. Pietersen, "Dialogical, Online Teaching," 133–47.

11. Coristine et al., "Student-teacher Relationships", para. 4.

12. Richardson and Langford, "Care-Full Pedagogy," 498–499.

encouragement from university teachers can make it difficult for students to remain engaged and motivated.[13]

However, if these decisions to engage students are executed well, the use of technology in online higher education and the care for students may yield long-lasting positive results beyond the online classroom.[14] The question then becomes: beyond the use of sophisticated technology to enhance teaching and learning, how can university teachers in online education spaces signal that genuine care is taking place?

4. HIDDEN COSTS OF NEGLECTING STUDENT ENGAGEMENT IN OPEN DISTANCE E-LEARNING

Pedagogies of care require thorough acknowledgement and engagement by university teachers with students from diverse backgrounds who may have access to technology, but may not be well versed in it. How is this brought to the fore? Although some students may have digital access and be tech savvy, others may lack access or familiarity with digital platforms, particularly in low-income communities. Therefore, it is essential for university teachers to acknowledge the challenges faced by such students, particularly in a digital environment where technology literacy is vital.[15]

However, some university teachers ignore this reality, assuming that all students are familiar with technology or can quickly adapt to new digital platforms. This assumption is misguided, as it fails to consider the unique challenges faced by students from diverse backgrounds. As a result, students who lack technology skills or digital access may feel left out, isolated, and frustrated, leading to a negative learning experience.[16] Students who struggle with technology may be at a disadvantage compared with their peers, particularly in a digital classroom. For example, they may

13. Hargreaves, "What COVID-19 Taught Us," 1835–63.
14. Lambrechts et al., "Decentralizing Emerging Markets," 111–53.
15. Williams et al., "AI+ Ethics Curricula," 1–59.
16. Ferri et al., "Online Learning," 86.

have difficulty accessing online resources, participating in group discussions, or submitting assignments on time. University teachers who refuse to acknowledge the struggles of these students can exacerbate the problem, leading to a lack of motivation and engagement among students.[17]

It is therefore crucial for university teachers to support students from diverse backgrounds who may be struggling with technology. This can be done by providing training or resources to help them improve their skills in digital literacy. University teachers can also use simple and user-friendly platforms and tools that are accessible to all students, regardless of their technical abilities.[18] Lecturers must make a deliberate choice to exercise a duty of care in online learning environments.[19] This is rooted in the understanding that students are more likely to flourish when technological tools are used not only for instruction but to support the development of the whole person. However, this can only be achieved when students, content, and university teachers engage meaningfully with one another. Moving beyond a standardized approach to online education—where sophisticated technology is present, but differentiation, expanded opportunities, and genuine student engagement are lacking—is essential. Without this, a pedagogy of care that attends to the student's holistic well-being is ultimately neglected.[20]

5. INFLUENCING TEACHER ATTITUDES TOWARDS STUDENTS IN OPEN DISTANCE e-LEARNING

The inequalities that shape and define students' lives often influence university teachers' attitudes toward them, sometimes in ways that undermine the quality of the student experience in online

17. DeCoito and Estaiteyeh, "Transitioning to Online Teaching," 340–56.

18. Coman et al., "Online Teaching and Learning," 10367.

19. Baker-Bell, "Dismantling Anti-black Linguistic Racism," 8–21.

20. Robinson et al., "Designing with Care," 99–108; Godsell, "Teaching Care," 1–23.

teaching and learning environments.[21] This raises a critical question for educators: how can they meaningfully enact their duty of care in the online space? Put differently, if university teachers are to fulfil their responsibility of care, they must reflect on the specific areas where that care is needed and how it can be effectively expressed to avoid failing their students.[22]

This kind of care can be located in two distinct places, namely agency (the student) and responsibility (the lecturer). In educational matters, this may be summarized as lecturers fulfilling their caregiving obligations, engaging in conversations around the distribution of their responsibilities, and guaranteeing that everyone can fully engage in those care distributions.[23]

This pedagogy of care can only be achieved successfully by lecturers in ODeL settings by first acknowledging students' habitus and then actively doing something about it to give greater recognition to disadvantaged students, rather than merely focusing on technology. In *Politics of Recognition*, Charles Taylor explains how social recognition has authenticity in human identity. Regarding teaching and learning in ODeL settings, it can be said that students may experience actual harm or distortion if university lecturers reflect back to them a limiting, degrading, or disdainful image of themselves. This is because our identity is partially formed by recognition or its absence, frequently by the misrecognition of others. Misrecognition or non-recognition can be harmful, oppressive, and confine someone in a diminished, distorted, and false way of being.[24]

Taylor's recognition theory extends to a multicultural society where all are equal and tolerant of one another and have access to the necessary resources to thrive. Where this research disagrees with Taylor is that in the education space, and particularly in online higher education, not all things are equal, because of our

21. Floyd, "Christian Higher Education," 371.
22. Neuwirth et al., "Reimagining Higher Education," 141–156.
23. Tronto, "Protective or Democratic Care?," 6.
24. Taylor, *Politics of Recognition*, 249–255.

colonialist past.[25] For instance, not all students are able to access higher education institutions, not many students have access to digital technology, and not many university teachers are open to engagement on these issues.

6. REDEFINING SUCCESS FOR FIRST-GENERATION STUDENTS IN OPEN DISTANCE E-LEARNING

In many South African higher education institutions, most students are first-generation students, 61% of them have been the first individuals in their family to attend a university, 7.05% have a mother that has already attended university, 3.32% a father, and 19.92% have had either a brother or sister attend a university before them.[26] These students, who have little or no family collegiate history, may enter the university with limited knowledge about the jargon, traditions, and patterns of expected behavior. These factors represent embedded inequalities and speak to a lack of resources and access that moves beyond the narrative of equal distribution.[27] However, Taylor's theory implies that multicultural recognition may need redistribution, particularly in education, because higher education is still largely for the advantaged, as indicated by the challenges in students' access to technology and resources. Therefore, if a care pedagogy is set against these issues, conditions may become far more bearable, enabling students to thrive and succeed in their studies.[28]

7. CONCLUSION

The goal of quality education envisaged by the 4IR must align with meaningful actions undertaken by all stakeholders in the teaching

25. Maigari, "Critique of Charles Taylor," 187–99.

26. Department of Higher Education and Training, *Students' Access to Learning Materials*, 53–80.

27. Gallo, "Bantu Education", 28–36.

28. Miller, "Hegemonic Whiteness," e12973.

and learning process. For developing ODeL institutions, it is therefore essential to adopt an action-reflection approach, one that not only reveals how students engage in online learning, but also highlights the importance of their personal narratives and diverse backgrounds in enriching the virtual classroom. This reflective cycle enables all participants in the teaching and learning process to improve and adjust their practices. Viewed through Freire's critical pedagogical lens, such an approach invites a deeper awareness of habitus in education and offers a pathway to embed a pedagogy of care in ODeL settings. Ultimately, this promotes a collaborative, socially just learning environment in which university educators and students across various disciplines can honor their cultural and historical identities, integrating them meaningfully into curriculum development and teaching practices.

CHAPTER 9

A Balancing Act Between a Pedagogy of Care, Students, and Academic Rigor in ODeL Environments

A pedagogy of care nurtures the being and becoming of students. One cannot teach careful practice without embedding and demonstrating care within the pedagogy itself, within the architectural studio. Care speaks to the respect, concern, consideration and sensitivity which we show ourselves and each other within.

—Sandra Felix

1. Introduction

The adoption of technological platforms should be used to benefit both the broader education system and the individual student, using a pedagogy of care approach.[1] The job of a good lecturer can be measured not only by how much students engage with class content, but also in the embodied cultural capital that students bring to online, face-to-face, and hybrid learning spaces. This requires that developing universities carefully manage the online teaching and learning space from an equity perspective to ensure

1. Haleem, "Digital Technologies in Education," 275–85.

that it does not result in inequalities being perpetuated due to students' diverse social backgrounds.

2. BALANCING CARE AND ACADEMIC RIGOR IN OPEN DISTANCE E-LEARNING

Tronto[2] posits that the teaching and learning process "starts from the premise that everything exists in relation to other things... and assumes that people, other beings, and the environment are interdependent." This includes providing students with opportunities to perform well by giving active feedback online and it addresses the notion that students can contribute to active learning.[3] It speaks to the fact that there exists some kind of level of care and engagement beyond just performing well academically on advanced online platforms.[4] This approach of support is critical to the teaching and learning environment provided in these online spaces.

Online teaching and learning can be understood through the lens of proportional care, where the extent to which university teachers care for students is limited. insofar as university teachers caring for students can be viewed as proportional. As Simon[5] suggests, the challenges academic staff face in digital learning environments may result in a form of "halfway" caring. This implies that university teachers are primarily interested in the descriptive aspects of course input and output, rather than engaging more holistically with students' learning experiences. Instead of merely analyzing how frequently students accessed content or the percentage breakdown of their responses, educators should seek to foster intrinsic motivation, encouraging active engagement and sustained participation among students. Such motivation encompasses both conscious (what we see) and unconscious (what we

2. Tronto, "Creating Caring Institutions," 158–71.
3. Gqokonqana et al., "Blended Learning Challenges," 87–107.
4. Makina, "Demotivating Online Assessment," 32–51.
5. Simon, *Impact of Online Teaching*, 19.

hear and feel) behavior.[6] A deliberate ethic of care is therefore essential in online education: it is an ongoing process that supports student success and promotes continuous progress in teaching and learning.

3. Empowering Students Through Collaborative Learning in Open Distance e-Learning

The level of perceived "realness" and interpersonal connection in online higher education is referred to as social presence. Establishing social presence is vital during lectures on digital platforms to address the lack of caring and dialogue which students feel.[7] This aligns with Freire's concept of teachers developing a caring atmosphere by actively engaging with students, encouraging meaningful connections, especially with marginalized students.[8] The educational process is largely centered on the student, giving them the opportunity to actively participate in their own learning. This strategy becomes essential in online education settings to overcome the perceived lack of concern and conversation.[9] By highlighting the significance of critical thinking, agency, and conversation to resist oppressive structures, Freire's theory is consistent with student-centered learning.

Teachers in online institutions can foster discussion, reflection, and collaboration by implementing student-centered approaches.[10] They can encourage students to express their opinions, pose questions, and take part in substantive debates regarding the social problems and power relations that are prevalent in their areas of study. This method not only encourages kindness and

6. Bekele, "Motivation and Satisfaction," 116–127.

7. Joosten, *Social Media for Educators*, 9–10; Picciano et al., *Blended Learning*, 200.

8. Benade, *Being a Teacher*, 205–6.

9. Sarwar et al., "Social Media for Collaborative Learning," 246–79; Papademetriou et al., "Social Media Technology," 261.

10. Rowley et al., "Student-led Pedagogic Approach," 35–45.

communication, but also gives young adults the tools they need to be proactive change agents.[11]

4. HUMANIZING STUDENT-CENTERED LEARNING IN OPEN DISTANCE E-LEARNING

In addressing the lack of care and dialogue in online higher education, the concepts of social presence, student-centered learning, and Freire's theory of the oppressed are important to grasp. Teachers humanize the online experience and create meaningful connections with their students by developing a social presence.[12] Student-centered learning encourages discussion and critical thinking, while giving students the freedom to participate actively in their education. This can be illustrated through the following figure:

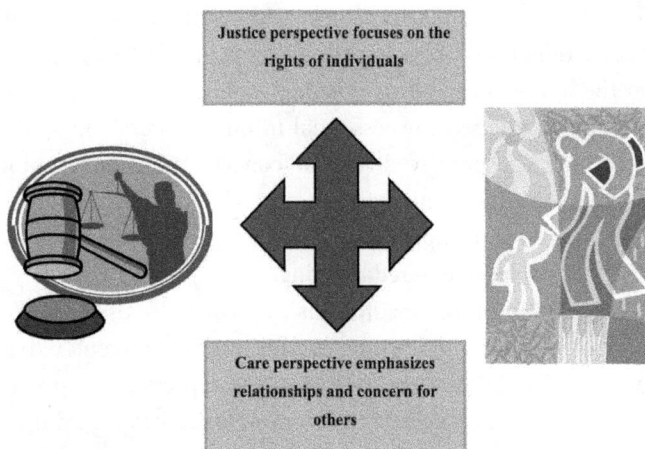

Justice perspective focuses on the rights of individuals

Care perspective emphasizes relationships and concern for others

Figure 4. Humanizing the Pedagogy of Care to Create Meaningful Connections with Students in an ODeL Framework

---

11. Mayo, *Gramsci, Freire and Adult Education*, 58–70; Kagan et al., *Critical Community Psychology*, 22.

12. Hirst and Brown, "Pedagogy as Dialogic Relationship," 179–99; Lyons and Tarc, "Promising Teacher Praxis," 1–20.

Humanizing the pedagogy of care in education involves fostering meaningful connections with students by prioritizing their emotional, social, and intellectual well-being, thereby creating an inclusive and supportive learning environment. A justice perspective, which focuses on the rights and equitable treatment of individuals, aligns with a pedagogy of care by ensuring that all students have access to the opportunities and resources necessary for their success.[13] Simultaneously, a care perspective emphasizes the importance of relationships, empathy, and concern for others, which are central to creating a sense of belonging and trust in educational settings.[14] These perspectives are interconnected within the pedagogy of care, as justice ensures structural fairness, while care nurtures the relational and emotional dimensions of learning. By integrating these approaches, educators can address systemic inequities, while also attending to the unique needs and experiences of individual students. This dual focus not only humanizes the learning process, but also empowers students to engage more deeply with their education, fostering a culture of mutual respect and shared responsibility. In practice, this might involve designing curricula that reflect diverse perspectives, providing personalized feedback, and creating spaces for dialogue that validate students' voices and experiences.

Incorporating Freire's philosophy into online higher education encourages both lecturers and students to resist oppressive structures and advocate for the well-being of marginalized groups.[15] By integrating such critical pedagogical approaches, developing online institutions can foster learning environments that are caring, dialogical, and empowering. These conditions not only support student agency, but also contribute to a more transformative and inclusive educational experience for all learners.

13. Hodges et al., "Remote Teaching and Online Learning," para. 4.

14. Noddings, "Caring Relation in Teaching," 771–81.

15. Cotter, "Global-local Connections," 91–100; Melvin et al., "Exploring Controversial Issues," 1–14.

5. CONCLUSION

This chapter examined how ODeL university instructors should work to improve the lives of their students and inculcate qualities that will greatly influence their future. This includes establishing a technologically stimulating online environment and crafting strategies to reach every student by treating them as individuals. The way social presence and student-centered learning perspectives interact in ODeL settings is one way of starting these important conversations. Put differently, lecturers should promote meaningful interactions with their students by implementing pedagogies of care and discourse.

Establishing universities in the ODeL space as transformational and socially just institutions requires careful consideration of multiple factors, particularly within technologically mediated environments where pedagogies of care are often overlooked. In the light of the significant increase in South African graduates since the end of apartheid, ODeL university instructors must remain attuned to the evolving social landscape and the complexities of a changing society. Creating a compassionate online teaching and learning environment in ODeL is therefore not optional, but essential. Genuine care and engagement fosters the whole person, rather than reducing higher education to the instrumental use of one-dimensional technological tools.

CHAPTER 10

Critical Pedagogical Action in ODeL Environments

Challenges and Opportunity for Caring

Caring for and about arguments, and the person who proffers them, are inextricably intertwined. It would be difficult not to care for a person; yet, caring also involves engaging seriously with the scholarly persuasion of the arguments made by a student.

—Yusef Waghid

1. INTRODUCTION

South African students' lives are interspersed with difficult encounters emanating from cultural embodiment, social disadvantages and stratified education which, taken together, present them with innumerable challenges.[1] These challenges were brought into sharp relief in the first nine weeks of the COVID-19 lockdown, which began on 27 March 2020 and required institutions of higher learning to quickly adapt and migrate their lessons to

---

1. Day, "Student Navigations," 67–80.

virtual platforms.[2] Exploring student experiences needs to be situated in ways to improve how lecturers ought to care for students who are in need of caring in ODeL environments and make it a more dialogical and democratic in order to uplift particularly marginalized students.[3]

This chapter aims to explore critical pedagogical action (specifically, dialogue and care) vis-à-vis the enactment of activism and justice among students in higher education. The author seeks to make sense of theoretical understandings in the context of real pedagogical action in ODeL online university classrooms.[4] Freire's pedagogy in particular extends the notion of dialogical engagement and caring for students, inspiring lecturers to deliberative action. Freire himself was epistemologically concerned with dialogical action which, together with his expansion into deliberative democratic theory, offers a different way of cultivating a socially just higher pedagogy.[5]

The student-lecturer relationship is subject to persistent interference in online higher education. This interference can take the form of the background students come from, lecturers' own cultural embodiment, technological barriers, including internet connectivity,[6] constant loadshedding, the cost of data, and various other inequalities. Even though cultivating a socially just higher pedagogy aimed at inclusion is a global phenomenon, I have chosen to focus on the South African online ODeL higher education context.

---

2. Elumalai et al., "Quality of e-Learning," 731–53.

3. Mhlanga et al., "Key Digital Transformation Lessons," 464.

4. Cornelius-Bell, "Student Activism," 338; Matthews and Dollinger, "Student Voice", 555–70.

5. Ngwoke and Ugwu, "Promoting Innovation," 37–8; Onah and Ugwu, "Kant's Thought Formation," 131–155.

6. Chukwuere, "Culture-oriented e-Learning," 70–8; Manase, *Exploring Experiences*, 25.

2. Care Ethic to Transform Learning in Open Distance e-Learning

1. In an online teaching and learning context, a lack of deep dialogical engagement and care between the lecturer and student remains an ongoing challenge.[7] This chapter evokes a critical dialogical pedagogy of caring to address the holistic needs of students on online teaching and learning platforms. A connection that is built on a care ethic that promotes communication is required for the type of online contact that takes place between lecturers and their students.[8]

2. This research also affirms that the cultural and socio-historical contexts of students and lecturers within online higher education are different. While it could be argued that some students share the same socioeconomic background of their lecturers, these are in the minority. The power wielded by lecturers over students, especially given the fact that they come from higher echelons of society, cannot be underestimated.

3. Botman[9] states that socio-political systems of domination in which elite, educated, and propertied lecturers hold power over students are disempowering in online higher education.[10] In analyzing lecturer education and development policy, Botman asserts that, despite a lot of effort and time having been invested in these processes, the principles of education praxis—namely, a practical pedagogy and an educational philosophy—had not been discussed or included.

The National Policy Framework for Teacher Education and Development, published in 2006, as well as higher education's teaching and learning policies, have been used and are still being wrongly

7. Sousa, "Dialogue in Online Learning," 229–37; Sedrakyan et al., "Feedback Digitalization Preferences," 56–75.

8. Pietersen, "Dialogical, Online Teaching," 133–47.

9. Botman, "Educators, Praxis and Hope," 84–5.

10. Mehta and Aguilera, "Humanizing Pedagogies," 109–20; Peercy et al., "Humanizing Principles," 1036–53.

interpreted to limit, disempower, and even perpetrate a lack of dialogue and uncaring attitudes towards students.[11] This is problematic because it has resulted in how society interprets the role and contributions of students in the country's socioeconomic development.

This research presents an opportunity for ODeL higher education institutions, including developing universities, to perceive their blind spots in how students are being treated on online teaching and learning platforms.[12] It is the researcher's conviction that as long as the problem exists, society can do something to rectify it.

3. Caring Reform in Teaching Policies for Student Empowerment in Open Distance e-Learning

My position as an ODeL lecturer in higher education has afforded me a unique perception of the problem under review. I have witnessed others, and even occasionally myself, falling into the trap of inadvertently treating students as subordinates. This is despite my deliberate attempts to engage in dialogue, democracy, and a pedagogy of care with students.[13] When I encountered difficulties, I reasoned that other lecturers might be struggling too, especially given how online teaching and learning in the wake of the pandemic made meaningful engagement with students more challenging. It was because of this that I set out to investigate the problem more thoroughly.

Higher education institutions have the power to change South Africa's educational history by altering the way that policy, teaching, and learning relationships are established. To do this, they

11. Lakey, *Facilitating Group Learning*, 25; Adams, "Pedagogical Foundations," 27–55.

12. Ovetz, "Algorithmic University," 1065–84; Ivancheva and Garvey, "Putting the University to Work," 381–97.

13. Nagda et al., "Transformative Pedagogy," 165–91; Carolissen and Kiguwa, "Narrative Explorations," 1–11.

must actively contribute to resolving the challenges that students face as they develop as citizens.[14] Educators should be conscious of how publicly visible their actions are, as stated by Botman.[15] It is worthwhile to share one's story if it promotes growth and development. This guides the way that policy documents on teaching and learning should be formulated. These policies on student support, engagement, and acre in ODeL higher education institutions should be read, reformed, and prioritized in order to support and integrate students' voices as active, well-informed, engaged members of their communities and of society as a whole.[16]

South African higher education institutions actively participate in the interpretation of educational approaches. Where these approaches are informed by the country's divided past, they should be interrogated and no longer be allowed to justify the exploitation of students. In this way, care and support for students will occur naturally in ODeL environments.

4. Embracing Diversity in Educational Practices in Open Distance e-Learning

As a lecturer at an ODeL university and a past primary and high school teacher, I have always aimed to create a caring educational environment where students from all backgrounds can flourish and feel valued. Taking students along on the learning journey and enabling them to dialogue and grow has been part of my pedagogical approach. The figure below indicates the undergirding philosophy of the Pietersen Intervention Framework (PIF), which is a behavioral perspective of instruction emphasizing action. This is important, so that a dialogical and caring pedagogy is not only cognitive, but that instruction is accompanied by change. Keeping this balance of the behavioral and cognitive approach enables lecturers to know what to do in classrooms. PIF's philosophy

14. Batisai, "Rethinking Inclusion," 210–230.

15. Botman, "Educators, Praxis and Hope," 86–7.

16. Nsamba, "Maturing Levels," 60–78; Sevnarayan, "Reimaging eLearning Technologies," 421–39.

envisions the implementation of dialogical and caring pedagogies in the following way:

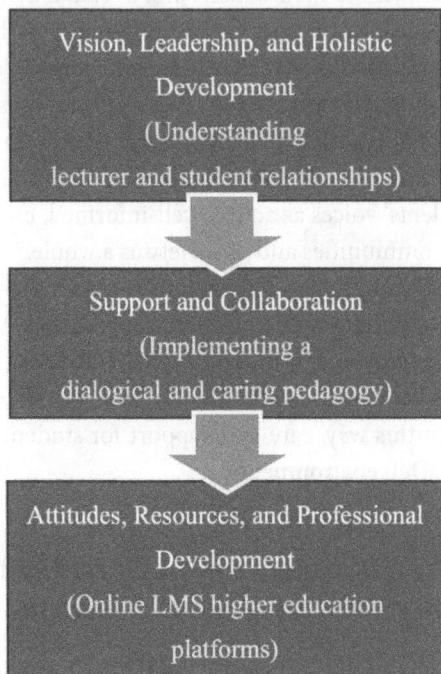

Figure 5. Transformational Steps for reading Pietersen Intervention Framework (PIF) into an ODeL Contexts

Pietersen's pedagogical approach is echoed by arguably the greatest educationalist of our time who asserts that the lecturer-of-the-students and the student-of-the-lecturer vanish through conversation and a new phrase—lecturer-student with students-lecturers—emerges.[17] The speaker is no longer just the teacher; he or she is also being taught by the students because they care and the students teach while being taught. They share accountability for a process that leads to everyone's growth. My approach is fore-grounded in an interpretivist view aligned with Freire to give students agency and voice in South African online higher education.

17. Frizelle, "Personal Is Pedagogical?," 17–35.

Dialogue reflects an informed praxis, but also underpins a transformative shift in pedagogical dynamics where hierarchical boundaries are replaced by reciprocal learning relationships.[18] This idea, rooted in Freirean dialogical pedagogy, emphasizes that education is a collaborative process in which both lecturers and students actively contribute to knowledge creation.[19] Recent scholarship highlights the importance of such reciprocal relationships in ODeL institutions, fostering inclusive and equitable learning environments, particularly in contexts where care and mutual respect are prioritized.[20] In this model, the lecturer is no longer the sole authority, but becomes a co-learner, guided by the insights and experiences of students. Simultaneously, students assume the role of educators, sharing their perspectives and challenging assumptions, thereby enriching the learning process for all participants in ODeL institutions.[21] This mutual accountability fosters a sense of shared responsibility for academic growth, aligning with the principles of a pedagogy of care, which emphasizes relationality and empathy.[22]

5. FREIRIAN DIALOGICAL PEDAGOGY AND ITS IMPORTANCE IN OPEN DISTANCE E-LEARNING

Freirean dialogical pedagogy can serve as a foundation for promoting inclusivity within the unfolding ODeL education system. This vision places the responsibility on educators to identify barriers to learning and offer support to students.[23] ODeL institutions of higher learning, including developing universities, should take responsibility for students who are silent because of their inherent

---

18. Pantazidis, "Commons-based Pedagogical Practices," 51.

19. Mudehwe, "Dialogic Pedagogic Innovation," 26–30; Dube and Mudehwe-Gonhovi, "Humanising Pedagogy," 147–166.

20. Rossi, *Inclusive Learning Design*, 35.

21. Robinson, "Student Engagement," 94–108; Mawonde and Togo, "Challenges Involving Students," 1487–502.

22. Hughes, "Caring, Community and Confrontation," 111.

23. Reed, "Critical Pedagogy," 26–30.

historical and social codes, and help them attain the same education as students who come with social capital.[24] Freire's pedagogy of dialogue and care enables lecturers in an ODeL environment to become more aware of their exclusionary practices and guide them towards becoming more inclusive. This is in line with the policy of White Paper 6, which aims at restructuring the South African education system in a way that promotes quality education for all. Experiencing democracy, dialogue, and care in online classrooms would enable universities to become more inclusive and supportive of their students.[25] It would also allow students to meaningfully share their stories and experiences, so that they can achieve their full potential and relate on an equal footing to their lecturers.

To embody Freirean leadership in educational spaces from which ODeL institutions can learn, lecturers must act as effective agents of change, empowering students to take responsibility for their actions and strive toward high academic standards.[26] But this approach provides opportunities for students as well, particularly in applying their knowledge both inside and outside of higher education.

In terms of vision, university management and lecturers need to be leaders in online higher education by understanding the curriculum and engaging in teaching and assessment in such a way that all students are supported and are allowed to give input.[27] In this way, students will have access to an improved standard of education and enjoy well-structured learning opportunities online.[28]

24. Mseleku, "Beyond Hard Barriers," 252–69.

25. Motala and Menon, "New Normal," 80–99.

26. Barnett and Teise, "Initial Teacher Education," 72–89.

27. Ruben et al., *Guide for Leaders*, 30.

28. Darling-Hammond et al., "Implications for Educational Practice," 97–140.

6. Implementing the Freirian Caring Pedagogy in Open Distance e-Learning

Institutions of higher learning in ODeL eco-systems, particularly developing universities, must recognize the complex social dynamics that shape teaching and learning in these environments. They must therefore have the resources and support that will enable them to meet the full range of learning and teaching needs among their students, including those who do not have online access. This can include investing in offline educational materials, such as printed resources or radio-based learning programs, to reach those without internet access. For example, the University of the Western Cape has initiated projects that distribute printed learning materials to students in remote areas, ensuring that they are not left behind in the digital age. Additionally, partnerships with local community centers can provide students with access to technology and internet facilities. By creating inclusive learning environments that acknowledge and address the complexities of social relations within ODeL spaces, institutions can foster a more equitable educational landscape. This comprehensive support not only enhances academic outcomes, but also empowers students to navigate their unique challenges, ultimately contributing to their personal and professional development.

ODeL institutions need to be open to receiving assistance in developing the capacity of lecturers and staff to incorporate a full range of teaching tools to address barriers to students' learning. This kind of input will need to pay special attention to developing flexibility in learning and teaching practices and styles through training, capacity building, and supporting both students and lecturers. This will also mean monitoring and evaluating how students and lecturers relate to each other on online teaching and learning platforms. The lessons learnt from this process should then be used to guide higher education institutions, but especially developing universities.

7. Institutional Support for Students from Diverse Backgrounds in Open Distance e-Learning

The key to removing and decreasing the number of barriers to dialogical and deliberate pedagogies of democracy in education lies in strengthening online educational support and caring for students. This requires a focused faculty teaching and learning manager who is equipped to deal with technological issues, as well as social interactions and especially caring for students. Such a support role needs to liaise with lecturers and students on the optimal use of ODeL platforms.[29]

In South Africa, where access to quality education has historically been unequal, enhancing online support can significantly bridge the gap for marginalized students.[30] For instance, institutions like the University of South Africa (UNISA) have implemented comprehensive online support services, including virtual learning environments that facilitate asynchronous discussions and collaborative projects. These platforms encourage dialogue among students, allowing them to share diverse perspectives and engage critically with course content in ODeL eco-systems.[31] By providing structured opportunities for interaction, universities empower students to take an active role in their learning, thereby promoting democratic values and participation in ODeL contexts.

Furthermore, integrating caring pedagogies into ODeL frameworks is vital for creating an inclusive and supportive educational atmosphere. Initiatives such as the South African Institute for Distance Education (SAIDE) emphasize the importance of personalized feedback and mentorship in online learning. By training educators to adopt a more empathetic approach, these initiatives help cultivate a sense of belonging among students who may feel isolated in digital environments.[32] For example, incor-

29. Munna and Kalam, "Teaching and Learning," 1–4.
30. Van Staden and Naidoo, "Future-proofing imperatives," 269–81.
31. Haley, "Unconventional Educational Approaches," 917–29.
32. Pacansky-Brock et al., "Humanizing Online Teaching," 1–21.

porating regular check-ins and providing mental health resources can foster stronger student-educator relationships, enhancing emotional support. Additionally, programs that encourage peer-support groups allow students to build networks of care and solidarity, which are essential for nurturing a collaborative learning culture. By prioritizing both educational support and emotional well-being, South African ODeL institutions can effectively dismantle barriers to dialogical and deliberative pedagogies, ultimately fostering a more democratic and participatory educational landscape.[33]

8. ATTITUDES AND BELIEFS TO FOSTER CARING IN OPEN DISTANCE E-LEARNING

What sets South African ODeL higher education apart from other countries' education systems is that historically it was based on apartheid, which involved racial attitudes towards those who were non-white (poor or working class) and the institutionalization of segregation.[34] It must be said that many countries have experienced difficulty in implementing inclusive education policies and South Africa is no different. However, only by possessing the will to change can true transformation occur. All lecturers in ODeL contexts, but particularly middle-class lecturers, need to be equipped with the right understanding that will foster students' engagement and success on online educational platforms.[35] Positive attitudes with regards to caregiving need to be introduced in virtual teaching and learning environments for lecturers to ensure that their students receive the quality education they deserve. Indeed, successful inclusion depends on the attitudes and actions in the education system as a whole.

Attitudes and beliefs are also culturally and socially embedded in ODeL eco-systems, as seen in Bourdieu's theory of cultural

---

33. Hibbert, *English as Language of Learning*, 25.

34. Mhonda, "Post-apartheid Economic and Education Reforms," 95.

35. Goudeau et al., "Lockdown and Distance Learning," 1273–81.

capital and Bernstein's code theory.[36] Therefore, the online community of an ODeL university needs to have an attitude that seeks to successfully implement inclusive education and allow students from working class backgrounds to flourish. A clear policy, together with the enforcement of such a policy, will be the most effective way to introduce and implement an effective online teaching and learning approach in an ODeL setting.[37] Strengthening the enforcement of such a policy will promote inclusion and the participation of students from various cultural and social backgrounds, so as to give credibility to the concept of *ubuntu*, especially in ODeL education environments.[38]

9. Directing Resources to Foster Caring in Open Distance e-Learning

To ensure student success in technology skills and proficiency with LMSes, developing universities in ODeL environments should collaborate closely with provincial education departments and local secondary schools, particularly to help upskill Grade 12 learners.[39] This speaks to deliberative, democratic education. As a first step, the teaching and learning departments at ODeL universities should include those schools that form part of the district development program and craft a strategy to teach digital skills to high-school learners.[40] This will empower these same learners when they become university students to keep lecturers accountable when caring pedagogies in ODeL education are not delivered. This process of teaching and learning in ODeL education spaces should be inclusive and deliberative, allowing students to be involved in the process of the visible and invisible curriculum formation right up to the implementation of teaching and learning

36. Claridge, *Social Capital and Cultural Capital*, 22.
37. Turnbull et al, "Transitioning to e-Learning," 6401–19.
38. Olawumi et al., "Situating Ubuntu," 605–23.
39. Mthabela, "Technical Vocational Education," 23.
40. Jung et al., "Digital Literacy Experiences," 41–59.

approaches.[41] In this manner, universities, including developing universities, will be able to expand the provision of digital skills to students within feeder-area schools that come from both working-class and severely impoverished backgrounds, so that no student is left behind.

To ensure that students are successful in their technology skills and knowledge of online platforms, it is essential for developing universities to collaborate closely with provincial departments of education and secondary schools. This partnership is particularly crucial for upskilling Grade 12 learners who are transitioning to ODeL higher education institutions. By implementing targeted training programs and workshops in secondary schools, educators can equip students with the necessary digital competencies and familiarity with LMS platforms before they enter higher education.[42] Such proactive measures not only enhance students' readiness for ODeL environments, but also foster a sense of agency and confidence in their ability to navigate digital learning spaces effectively. This collaborative approach aligns with the principles of deliberative, democratic education where educational stakeholders actively engage in dialogue and collective decision-making to create equitable learning pathways in ODeL environments.[43]

Furthermore, this emphasis on upskilling resonates with the philosophy of caring pedagogies, which prioritize the holistic development of students within educational contexts. In ODeL settings, where physical interaction with instructors may be limited, nurturing a supportive and empathetic learning environment becomes even more critical.[44] By integrating caring pedagogies into the curriculum and training programs, ODeL universities can promote an inclusive atmosphere that values students' diverse backgrounds and experiences.[45] This approach not only addresses

41. Parker and Bickmore, "Classroom Peace Circles," 103129.

42. Carabregu-Vokshi et al., "21st century Digital Skills," 103–137.

43. Bates and O'Connor Bones, "Community Conversations," 45.

44. Tripon et al., "Nurturing Minds," 9349.

45. Darawong and Sandmaung, "Service Quality Enhancing Student Satisfaction," 268–283.

the technical aspects of learning, but also emphasizes emotional and social dimensions, fostering a community of learners who feel valued and understood. As Grade 12 learners transition into ODeL institutions, such collaborative efforts between secondary schools and universities can nurture a culture of care and support, ultimately enhancing students' academic success and personal growth in their ODeL higher education journey.[46]

10. PROFESSIONAL DEVELOPMENT TO FOSTER CARING IN OPEN DISTANCE E-LEARNING

Human resource development for lecturers is the primary means for achieving the goal of inclusive ODeL education and training systems for students taught on online platforms. Lecturers need to be required to improve their skills and knowledge, and develop new perspectives on their study guide content,[47] as well as their methods of teaching, specifically with regards to fostering positive pedagogical action. Academic staff development at a faculty level will be critical to implement successful, integrated, online teaching and learning educational practices. Ongoing assessments of lecturers' needs, followed by structured programs to meet those needs, are incredibly important to implementing inclusion and deliberative caring pedagogies for students.[48]

Prioritizing professional development in the ODeL teaching and learning environment will give rise to a multilevel online instruction, so that lecturers can prepare main lessons with diversions that are responsive to individual student's needs and provide varied input.[49] This will result in cooperative learning, curriculum enrichment, and addressing students with behavioral challenges. This should not exclude management and governance

---

46. Saidi, "Enhancing Academic Success," 1–19; Gredley, "Socially Just Pedagogies," 43–5.

47. Hove and Phasha, "Support Services for Learners," 1–10.

48. Al Amri, "Integrating Care Pedagogy," 9–13.

49. Sims and Fletcher-Wood, "Effective Teacher Professional Development," 47–63.

development programs, which may wish to record data that will be needed to review and alter their online pedagogical approach. These interventions will sustain excellent dialogical outcomes and will create a sense of deliberative democracy in students' ODeL educational formation. If this is done well, students will feel that they are included in ODeL universities, cared for, and that they will ultimately flourish in the online education space.[50]

11. CONCLUSION

ODeL education has been impacted by the external environment, namely the Fourth Industrial Revolution, COVID-19 and the uncertain learning and teaching environment. This foregrounds the importance of deliberative democracy within higher education. The use of a strong LMS platform in ODeL environments must be inclusive of students whose socioeconomic and cultural backgrounds differ from lecturers'. Consequently, the question of democracy in online education will give insights as to how higher education institutions, such as ODeL universities, can positively respond to ever-changing external and internal dynamics. Therefore, it should be a prerequisite for lecturers to engage with their students in ODeL settings culturally, socially, psychologically, and even politically in order to groom them for success in their studies and in later life.

50. Ferri et al., "Online Learning," 86.

Bibliography

Abbas, Andrea, and Monica McLean. "Tackling Inequality through Quality: A Comparative Case Study Using Bernsteinian Concepts." *Global Inequalities and Higher Education* 6, no. 16 (2016): 241–67.

Adams, Fareed, and Yusef Waghid. "In Defence of Deliberative Democracy: Challenging Less Democratic School Governing Body Practices." *South African Journal of Education* 25, no. 1 (2005): 25–33.

Adams, Maurianne, et al. "Pedagogical Foundations for Social Justice Education." In *Teaching for Diversity and Social Justice*, 27–55. London: Routledge, 2022.

Adinda, Dina, and Najoua Mohib. "Teaching and Instructional Design Approaches to Enhance Students' Self-Directed Learning in Blended Learning Environments." *Electronic Journal of e-Learning* 18, no. 2 (2020): 162–74.

Ahmed, Sayem, et al. "Evaluation of flexible strategies to manage the COVID-19 pandemic in the education sector." *Global Journal of Flexible Systems Management* (2021), 1–25.

Aina, Carmen, et al. "The Determinants of University Dropout: A Review of the Socioeconomic Literature." *Socioeconomic Planning Sciences* 79 (2022): 101102.

Ajoodha, Ritesh, et al. "Forecasting Learner Attrition for Student Success at a South African University." In *Conference of the South African Institute of Computer Scientists and Information Technologists* (2020), 19–28.

Akuffo, Maxwell N., and Stephen Budu. "Use of Electronic Resources by Students in a Premier Postgraduate Theological University in Ghana." South African Journal of Information Management 21, no. 1 (2019): 1–9.

Al Amri, Kamla S. "Guidelines for Integrating Care Pedagogy into Faculty Development for Future Emergency Remote Teaching (ERT) in Higher Education: The CARE Framework." PhD diss, Virginia Polytechnic Institute and State University, 2025.

Alam, Ashraf, and Atasi Mohanty. "Educational Technology: Exploring the Convergence of Technology and Pedagogy through Mobility, Interactivity, AI, and Learning Tools." *Cogent Engineering* 10, no. 2 (2023): 2283282.

Bibliography

Albulescu, Ion, and Ciprian Simut. "The Importance of Human Rights Education in Developing Democratic Citizens." *Journal for Freedom of Conscience (Jurnalul Libertății de Conștiință)* 12, no. 3 (2024): 167–87.

Alexander, Robin. *A Dialogic Teaching Companion.* London: Routledge, 2020.

Alger, Mari and June Eyckmans, 2023. "Positive Surprises and Particular Struggles: A Case Study Exploring Students' Adjustment to Emergency Online Learning and Associated Emotions." In *Optimizing Online English Language Learning and Teaching,* 53–84. Cham: Springer International Publishing.

Alsaleh, Nada J. "Teaching Critical Thinking Skills: Literature Review." *Turkish Online Journal of Educational Technology-TOJET* 19, no. 1 (2020): 21–39.

Altes, Tisja K., et al. "Higher Education Teachers' Understandings of and Challenges for Inclusion and Inclusive Learning Environments: A Systematic Literature Review." Educational Research Review, no. 100605 (2024).

Alyoussef, Ibrahim Y. "The Impact of Massive Open Online Courses (MOOCs) on Knowledge Management Using Integrated Innovation Diffusion Theory and the Technology Acceptance Model." Education Sciences 13, no. 6 (2023): 531.

Anderson, L. M. and F. H. Taylor, F. H. *Sociology: Understanding a Diverse Society.* Belmont: Thomson Wadsworth, 2006.

Anyon, Jean. "Social Class and the Hidden Curriculum of Work." In *Childhood Socialization,* 369–94. London: Routledge, 2017.

Armonda, Alex J. "In Freire More Than Freire: Towards a New Psychoanalytic Foundation for Critical Pedagogy." The University of Texas at Austin, 2022.

Arnot, Madeleine, and Diane Reay. "Power, Pedagogic Voices and Pupil Talk: The Implications for Pupil Consultation as Transformative Practice." In *Knowledge, Power and Educational Reform: Applying the Sociology of Basil Bernstein.* London: Routledge, 2006.

Asamoah, M. K. "Sturdiness and scuffle in deploying educational technologies for teaching and learning in a low-technology context: Students' experience in a developing society. *African Journal of Science, Technology, Innovation and Development* 13, no. 2 (2021), 167–84.

Asterhan, Christa S. C., et al. "Controversies and Consensus in Research on Dialogic Teaching and Learning." *Dialogic Pedagogy* 8 (2020): 1–16.

Attard, Angele, et al. "Student-Centered Learning: Toolkit for Students, Staff and Higher Education Institutions". European Students' Union (NJ1), 2010.

Avram, Silvia and Jaap Dronkers, J. "Social class dimensions in the selection of a private school: a cross-national analysis using PISA. *Educational Research and Evaluation* 16, no. 2 (2005): 1–17.

Badaru, K. A. and E. O. Adu. "Platformisation of Education: An Analysis of South African Universities' Learning Management Systems." *Research in Social Sciences and Technology* 7, no. 2 (2022): 66–86.

Bibliography

Bailin, Sharon, and Mark Battersby. *Critical Thinking: A User's Manual*. London: Routledge, 2016.

Baker, Sally, et al. "COVID-19 Online Learning Landscapes and CALDMR Students: Opportunities and Challenges." National Centre for Student Equity in Higher Education, 2022.

Baker-Bell, April. 2020. "Dismantling anti-black linguistic racism in English language arts classrooms: Toward an antiracist black language pedagogy." *Theory into Practice* 59, no. 1 (2020): 8–21.

Ballantine, Jeanne, et al. *The Sociology of Education: A Systematic Analysis*. London: Routledge, 2021.

Ballim, Yunis. "T. B. Davie Academic Freedom Lecture." Lecture presented at the University of Cape Town, hosted by the Academic Freedom Committee, August 25, 2021.

Baloran, Erick, et al. "Course Satisfaction and Student Engagement in Online Learning Amid COVID-19 Pandemic: A Structural Equation Model." *Turkish Online Journal of Distance Education* 22, no. 4 (2021): 1–12.

Barnett, E. P., and K. Teise. "Initial Teacher Education for Social Justice in South Africa: A Higher Education Policy Perspective." *Research in Educational Policy and Management* 6, no. 1 (2024), 72–89.

Barrot, J. S. and A. R. R. Fernando. "Unpacking engineering students' challenges and strategies in a fully online learning space: The mediating role of teachers." *Education and Information Technologies* (2023), 1–23.

Bartlett, Steve, and Burton, Diana. *Introduction to Education Studies*. Thousand Oaks, CA: Sage Publishing, 2024.

Basar, Z. M., et al. "The Effectiveness and Challenges of Online Learning for Secondary School Students–A Case Study." *Asian Journal of University Education* 17, no. 3 (2021): 119–29.

Bastos, Flàvia, and Doug Blandy, eds. *Promoting Civic Engagement Through Art Education: A Call to Action for Creative Educators*. Milton Park, UK: Taylor & Francis, 2024.

Bates, J., and U. O'Connor Bones. "Community Conversations: deliberative democracy, education provision and divided societies." *SN Social Sciences* 1, no. 2 (2021): 45.

Batisai, K., et al. "Rethinking inclusion in higher education: Lessons for the South African academic space." *South African Journal of Higher Education*, 36, no. 6, 210–230.

Bayot, Marlon L., et al. "Human Subjects Research Design." In *StatPearls*. Treasure Island, FL: StatPearls Publishing, 2023.

Bazana, Sandiso, and Opelo P. Mogotsi. "Social Identities and Racial Integration in Historically White Universities: A Literature Review of the Experiences of Black Students." *Transformation in Higher Education* 2 (2017): 25.

Beckett, Linnea K., et al. "Beyond Inclusion: Cultivating a Critical Sense of Belonging through Community-Engaged Research." *Social Sciences* 11, no. 3 (2022): 132.

Bibliography

Bekele, T. A. "Motivation and satisfaction in internet-supported learning environments: A review." *Journal of Educational Technology and Society* 13, no. 2 (2010): 116–127.

Benade, Leon. *Being a Teacher in the 21st century. A Critical New Zealand Research Study.* London: Springer Nature, 2017.

Benson, Lee, et al. *Dewey's Dream: Universities and Democracies in an Age of Education Reform: Civil Society, Public Schools, and Democratic Citizenship.* Temple University Press, 2007.

Bernstein, Basil. *Pedagogy, Symbolic Control and Identity: Theory, Research, Critique.* Lanham, MD: Rowman and Littlefield, 2000.

———. *Class, Codes and Control: Applied Studies Towards a Sociology of Language.* London: Psychology Press, 2003.

———. "Language and Social Class." *The British Journal of Sociology* 11, no. 3 (1960): 271–76.

Bertram, Carol. "Bernstein's Theory of the Pedagogic Device as a Frame to Study History Curriculum Reform in South Africa." *Yesterday and Today,* School of Education, University of KwaZulu-Natal, 2012.

Bhana, Deevia. "Race Matters and the Emergence of Class: Views from Selected South African University Students." *South African Journal of Higher Education* 28, no. 2 (2014): 355–67.

Biesta, Gert. "Interrupting the Politics of Learning." *Power and Education* 5, no. 1 (2013): 4–15.

Bloch, Graeme. *Building Education Beyond Crisis: Development Today.* Johannesburg: Development Bank of Southern Africa, 2005.

Boluk, K., and Carnicelli, S. Tourism for the emancipation of the oppressed: Towards a critical tourism education drawing on Freirean philosophy. *Annals of Tourism Research* 76 (2019), 168–179.

Bond, Melissa, et al. "Mapping Research in Student Engagement and Educational Technology in Higher Education: A Systematic Evidence Map." *International Journal of Educational Technology in Higher Education* 17 (2020): 1–30.

Bosio, E. Global South University Educators' Perceptions of Global Citizenship Education: Reflective dialogue, social change, and critical awareness. *PROSPECTS* (2023), 1–15.

Botman, B. V. "Educators, Praxis and Hope: A Philosophical Analysis of Post-Apartheid Teacher Education Policy." PhD diss., Stellenbosch University, 2014.

Bough, Ashley and Gabriela Martinez Sainz. "Digital learning experiences and spaces: Learning from the past to design better pedagogical and curricular futures". *The Curriculum Journal* 34, no. 3 (2022): 375–393.

Bourdieu, Pierre. "The Forms of Capital." In *Handbook of Theory and Research for the Sociology of Education,* edited by John G. Richardson, 241–58. New York: Greenwood Press, 1986.

Bovill, Catherine, et al. *Co-Creating Learning and Teaching: Towards Relational Pedagogy in Higher Education.* London: Routledge, 2025.

Bibliography

Bowden, Jana L. H., et al. "The Four Pillars of Tertiary Student Engagement and Success: A Holistic Measurement Approach." *Studies in Higher Education* 46, no. 6 (2021): 1207–24.

Bowles, Samuel, and Herbert Gintis. *Schooling in Capitalist America*. New York: Basic Books, 1976.

Bozalek, Vivienne, and Michalinos Zembylas. "Diffraction or Reflection? Sketching the Contours of Two Methodologies in Educational Research." *International Journal of Qualitative Studies in Education* 30, no. 2 (2017): 111–27.

Bozkurt, Aras, et al. "Openness in Education as a Praxis: From Individual Testimonials to Collective Voices." *Open Praxis* 15, no. 2 (2023): 76–112.

Brantlinger, Ellen. *Dividing Classes: How the Middle Class Negotiates and Rationalizes School Advantage*. New York: Routledge, 2013.

Brevik, Lisbeth M., et al. "Student Teachers' Practice and Experience with Differentiated Instruction for Students with Higher Learning Potential." *Teaching and Teacher Education* 71 (2018): 34–45.

Brown, Kate. *Vulnerability and Young People: Care and Social Control in Policy and Practice*. Bristol: Policy Press, 2016.

Buchanan, John. Improving the Quality of Teaching and Learning: A Teacher-as-learner-centred Approach. *International Journal of Learning* 18, no. 10 (2012): 345–56.

Buchanan, Rachel, et al. "Philosophy of Education in a New Key: Exploring New Ways of Teaching and Doing Ethics in Education in the 21st Century." *Educational Philosophy and Theory* 54, no. 8 (2022): 1178–97.

Burger, Kaspar. "Human Agency in Educational Trajectories: Evidence from a Stratified System." *European Sociological Review* 37, no. 6 (2021): 952–71.

Burke, Catherine. "Capitals and Habitus: A Bourdieusian Framework for Understanding Transitions into Higher Education and Student Experiences." In *Access to Higher Education*, edited by Anna Mountford-Zimdars and Neil Harrison, 65–80. London: Routledge, 2016.

Burke, K and S. Larmar. "Acknowledging Another Face in the Virtual Crowd: Reimagining the Online Experience in Higher Education through an Online Pedagogy of Care." *Journal of Further and Higher Education* 45, no. 5 (2021): 601–615.

Caetano, Ana P., et al. "Student Voice and Participation in Intercultural Education." *Journal of New Approaches in Educational Research* 9, no. 1 (2020): 57–73.

Calarco, Jessica M. *Negotiating Opportunities: How the Middle Class Secures Advantages in School*. Oxford: Oxford University Press, 2018.

Carabregu-Vokshi, M., et al. "21st century digital skills of higher education students during Covid-19—is it possible to enhance digital skills of higher education students through E-Learning?" *Education and Information Technologies* 29, no. 1 (2024), 103–137.

Carolissen, R., and P. Kiguwa. "Narrative explorations of the micro-politics of students' citizenship, belonging and alienation at South African

Bibliography

universities." *South African Journal of Higher Education* 32, no. 3 (2018), 1–11.

Carter Andrews, D. J., et al. "A call to action for teacher preparation programs: Supporting critical conversations and democratic action in safe learning environments." *Journal of Teacher Education* 69, no. 3 (2018), 205–8.

Cassandra, Nina W., et al. "Enacting Dialogic Pedagogy in an EFL Online Classroom: A Self-Study." *Studying Teacher Education* (2024): 1–23.

Cele, Siyanda M. K., et al. "Black African Students' Social and Academic Identities in South African Universities Vis-à-Vis Student Dropout: A Social Justice and Philosophical Perspective." *Journal of Culture and Values in Education* 8, no. 1 (2025): 240–51.

Chan, Cecelia K. Y., and Wenjie Hu. "Students' Voices on Generative AI: Perceptions, Benefits, and Challenges in Higher Education." *International Journal of Educational Technology in Higher Education* 20, no. 1 (2023): 43.

Chiramba, Otilia, and Elizabeth S. Ndofirepi. "Access and Success in Higher Education: Disadvantaged Students' Lived Experiences Beyond Funding Hurdles at a Metropolitan South African University." *South African Journal of Higher Education* 37, no. 6 (2023): 56–75.

Chirinda, B., et al. "Teaching mathematics during the COVID-19 lockdown in a context of historical disadvantage." *Education Sciences* 11, no. 4 (2021): 177.

Choo, L. P., et al. "Patterns of interaction among ESL students during online collaboration." *Procedia-Social and Behavioral Sciences* 123 (2014), 307–14.

Chukwuere, J. E. "Towards a culture-oriented e-Learning System Development Framework in higher education institutions in South Africa." PhD diss., North-West University, 2016.

Cicha, Karina, et al. "COVID-19 and Higher Education: First-year Students' Expectations toward Distance Learning." *Sustainability* 13, no. 4 (2021): 80–89.

Claridge, Tristan. *The Difference between Social Capital and Cultural Capital*. Brisbane: Institute for Social Capital, 2022.

Cohen, Louis, et al. The Ethics of Educational and Social Research. In *Research Methods in Education*, 111–143. London: Routledge, 2017.

Cole, Mike, ed. *Education, Equality and Human Rights: Issues of Gender, Race, Sexuality, Disability and Social Class*. New York: Taylor & Francis, 2022.

Coman, Claudiu, et al. Online teaching and learning in higher education during the coronavirus pandemic: Student's perspective. *Sustainability* 12, no. 24 (2020): 10367.

Cook-Sather, Alison. "Respecting Voices: How the Co-Creation of Teaching and Learning Can Support Academic Staff, Underrepresented Students, and Equitable Practices." *Higher Education* 79, no. 5 (2020): 885–901.

Coristine, S., et al. "The importance of student-teacher relationships. Classroom practise in 2022." [Accessed March 2022].

Bibliography

Coristine, S., et al. *The importance of student-teacher relationships*. Classroom Practice, April 1, 2022. https://ecampusontario.pressbooks.pub/educ5202/ chapter/the-importance-of-student-teacher-relationships/

Cornelius-Bell, Aidan. "Student activism in higher education: The politics of students' role in hegemonic university change." PhD diss, Flinders University, 2021.

Costa, Cristina, and Mark Murphy. *Bourdieu, Habitus and Social Research, the Art of Application*. London: Palgrave Macmillan, 2015.

Cotter, G. "Global-local connections: what educators, who use community-linked and multimedia methodologies, can learn about critically engaging university students in development education." PhD diss., University College Cork, 2019.

Cross, Michael, and Vivian Atinde. "The pedagogy of the marginalized: Understanding how historically disadvantaged students negotiate their epistemic access in a diverse university environment." *Review of Education, Pedagogy, and Cultural Studies* 37, no. 4 (2015), 308–25.

Czerniewicz, Laura, et al. "A Wake-up Call: Equity, Inequality and COVID-19 Emergency Remote Teaching and Learning." *Post-digital Science and Education* (2020): 946–67.

Daniels, Michael A., and Gary J. Greguras. Exploring the nature of power distance: Implications for micro-and macro-level theories, processes, and outcomes. *Journal of Management* 40, no. 5 (2015): 1202–29.

Daniels, Nadia M., et al. "South African New Academics' Experiences of Precarity: Becoming and Unbecoming the Condition of Coloniality through Collective Reflexivity." *Critical Studies in Teaching and Learning (CriSTaL)* 12, no. 1 (2024): 40–62.

Darawong, C., and Sandmaung, M. (2019). "Service quality enhancing student satisfaction in international programs of higher education institutions: A local student perspective." *Journal of Marketing for Higher Education* 29, no. 2 (2019), 268–283.

Darder, Antonia, et al. "Critical Pedagogy: An Introduction." In *The Critical Pedagogy Reader*, 1–30. New York: Routledge, 2023.

Darling-Hammond, Linda, et al. "Implications for Educational Practice of the Science of Learning and Development." *Applied Developmental Science* 24, no. 2 (2020): 97–140.

Davids, Nuraan, and Yusef Waghid. "Coda: Democratic Citizenship Education and the Notion of 'Bare Life'." In *African Democratic Citizenship Education Revisited*, 221–30. London: Palgrave Macmillan, 2018.

Day, Helen. "Philanthropy, Scholarships and Student navigations in a changing South African educational landscape." PhD diss., University of Cape Town, 2023.

De Clercq, Francine. "The persistence of South African educational inequalities: The need for understanding and relying on analytical frameworks." *Education as Change* 24, no. 1 (2020), 1–22.

Bibliography

De Klerk, Danie. "Academic Advising and Ethic of Care: Enabling Belonging to Enhance Higher Education Students' Prospects of Success." *South African Journal of Higher Education* 36, no. 6 (2022): 152–68.

De Moll, Frederick, et al. "Students' Academic Habitus and Its Relation to Family Capital: A Latent Class Approach to Inequalities among Secondary School Students 1." *Sociological Inquiry* 94, no. 1 (2024), 190–220.

DeCoito, I., and M. Estaiteyeh. 2022. Transitioning to online teaching during the COVID-19 pandemic: An exploration of the views, successes, and challenges of STEM teachers. *Journal of Science Education and Technology* 31, no. 3 (2022): 340–56.

Demir, Ema K. The role of social capital for teacher professional learning and student achievement: A systematic literature review. *Educational Research Review* 33 (2021): 100391.

Demirbolat, A. O. *The Relationship between Democracy and Education.* Sharjah: Bentham Science Publishers, 2012.

Denzin, Norman K. and Yvonna S. Lincoln, eds. *The SAGE Handbook of Qualitative Research.* Thousand Oaks, CA: SAGE Publications, 2017.

Department of Higher Education and Training. *Students' Access to and Use of Learning Materials.* Pretoria, Republic of South Africa: 2020.

Devine, C. "Socratic Circles Pedagogy: Dialogue About and Demonstration of Values." In *Second International Research Handbook on Values Education and Student Wellbeing,* 1053–69. Cham: Springer International Publishing, 2023.

Dewey, John. *Democracy and Education.* Columbia University Press, 2024.

Dhungana, Parbati. "A Critical-Appreciative Approach as/for Transformative Professional Development." *International Journal of Multidisciplinary Perspectives in Higher Education* 6, no. 2 (2021): 156–81.

Dias, B. B., et al. "DeepLMS: A Deep Learning Predictive Model for Supporting Online Learning in the Covid-19 era." *Scientific Reports* 10, no. 1 (2020): 1–17.

Ditaunyane, S. E. "The Integration of Multimedia Resources in the Teaching of Tswana at Secondary Schools in the Motheo District." PhD diss., University of Stellenbosch, 2008.

Dixon, R., et al. "Online student-centred discussion: Creating a collaborative learning environment. Hello! Where are you in the landscape of educational technology?" Proceedings ascilite Melbourne, 2008.

Dombaycı, Mehmet A. "Philosophy for Children and Social Inquiry: An Example of Education for Democratic Citizenship Through Political Philosophy." *Cumhuriyet International Journal of Education* 3, no. 2 (2014): 85–101.

Doyle, Terry. *Helping students learn in a learner-centered environment: A guide to facilitating learning in higher education.* Milton Park, UK: Taylor & Francis, 2023.

Bibliography

Drury, Sara A. M., et al. "Assessing Deliberative Pedagogy: Using a Learning Outcomes Rubric to Assess Tradeoffs and Tensions." *Journal of Deliberative Democracy* 12, no. 1 (2016).

Dube, N., and Mudehwe-Gonhovi, F. R. (2022). Humanising Pedagogy and International Students' Adjustment at an Institution of Higher Learning in South Africa. *Journal of Educational Studies*, 21, no. 1 (2022), 147–166.

Edgerton, Jason D., and Lance W. Roberts. "Cultural capital or habitus? Bourdieu and beyond in the explanation of enduring educational inequality." *Theory and Research in Education* 12, no. 2 (2014): 193–220.

Elumalai, Kesavan V., et al "Factors affecting the quality of e-learning during the COVID-19 pandemic from the perspective of higher education students." *Journal of Information Technology Education: Research* 19 (2020): 731–53.

Englund, Tomas. "Higher Education, Democracy and Citizenship: The Democratic Potential of the University?" *Studies in Philosophy and Education* 21 (2002): 281–87.

Escobar, J. D. E., et al. "Reading Reality through Dialogue for the Development of Paulo Freire's Critical Pedagogy." *Contemporary Readings in Law and Social Justice* 16 (2024): 929.

Farooq, Sana. "The Critically Reflective Practice of Online Educators: Constructing a Dialogic Pedagogy in Virtual Learning Environments." *Academia*, 2019.

Fataar, Aslam. "Pedagogical justice and student engagement in South African schooling: Working with the cultural capital of disadvantaged students." *Perspectives in Education* 30, no. 4 (2012), 52–75.

———. "Introducing the Terms of Mis(recognition) in Respect of Students' Educational Practices across Power Marginalised Spaces." *The Educational Practices and Pathways of South African Students across Power Marginalised Spaces* (2018). 7–18.

Fataar, Aslam and Norodien-Fataar, Najwa. "Toward an e-learning ecologies approach to pedagogy in a post-COVID world." *Journal of Education* 84 (2021): 155–68.

Feldman, J. 2020. An Ethics of Care: PGCE students' experiences of online learning during Covid-19. Critical Studies in Teaching and Learning (CriSTaL), 8(2): 1–17.

Felix, S. L. "Tracing the evolution of a parallel-engaged architectural pedagogy of care in South Africa." *Archnet-IJAR: International Journal of Architectural Research* (2024).

Ferri, Fernando, et al. "Online Learning and Emergency Remote Teaching: Opportunities and Challenges in Emergency Situations." *Societies* 10, no. 4 (2020): 86.

Fine, Ben. *Theories of Social Capital: Researchers Behaving Badly.* London: Pluto Press, 2010.

Floyd, S., et al. "Introduction to the theme issue: Christian Higher Education as Character Formation." *Christian Scholar's Review* 39, no 4 (2010): 371.

Bibliography

Foucault, Michel. "Questions of Method." In *The Foucault Effect: Studies in Governmentality*, edited by G. Burchell, et al., 73–87. Chicago: University of Chicago Press, 1991.

———. "The Subject and Power." *Critical Inquiry* 8, no. 4 (1982): 777–95.

Fouche, I., and Andrews, G. "'Working from home is one major disaster': An analysis of student feedback at a South African university during the Covid-19 lockdown." *Education and Information Technologies* 27, no. 1 (2022): 133–55.

Freire, Paulo. *Pedagogy of the Oppressed*. Translated by Myra B. Ramos. Freiburg, Germany: Herder, 1972.

———. *Pedagogy of the Oppressed, 50th Anniversary Edition*. London: Bloomsbury Academic, 2018.

———. *Pedagogy of Freedom: Ethics, Democracy, and Civic Courage*. Lanham, MD: Rowman and Littlefield Publishers, 2000.

Freire, Paulo, et al. *Teachers as Cultural Workers: Letters to Those Who Dare Teach*. London: Routledge. 2005.

Frizelle, K. L. "The personal is pedagogical (?): Personal narratives and embodiment as teaching strategies in higher education." *South African Journal of Higher Education* 34, no. 2 (2020), 17–35.

Gabel, Susan. "Some conceptual problems with critical pedagogy." *Curriculum Inquiry* 32, no. 2 (2002): 177–201.

Galbin, Alexandra. "An Introduction to Social Constructionism." *Social Research Reports* 1, no. 2 (2014): 82–92.

Gallo, Matthew A. "Bantu education and its living educational and socioeconomic legacy in apartheid and post-apartheid South Africa." PhD diss., Fordham University, 2020.

García-Carrión, Rocío, et al. "Implications for Social Impact of Dialogic Teaching and Learning." *Frontiers in Psychology* 11, no. 140 (2020): 1–11.

Garrison, D. R., and Heather Kanuka. "Blended Learning: Uncovering Its Transformative Potential in Higher Education." *The Internet and Higher Education* 7, no. 2 (2004): 95–105.

Garrison, D. R., and Terry Anderson. *E-Learning in the 21st Century: A Community of Inquiry Framework for Online Learning*. London: Routledge, 2003.

Gasa, Velisiwe. "The Implications of the Digital Divide on Rural Students Enrolled in Open and Distance E-learning Institutions." *Conrado Journal* 20, no. 101 (2024), 562–7.

Giroux, Henry A. *Theory and Resistance in Education: Towards a Pedagogy for the Opposition*. London: Bloomsbury Publishing, 2024.

Godsell, S. "Teaching Care During Covid-19: Reflective Assessment for Becoming Historians." *Education as Change* 26, no. 1 (2022): 1–23.

Gordon, C. T. "Trusting Students' Voices in Critical English Education." *Journal of Language and Literacy Education* 15, no. 1 (2019): 1–32.

Bibliography

Goudeau, S., et al. "Why lockdown and distance learning during the COVID-19 pandemic are likely to increase the social class achievement gap." *Nature Human Behaviour* 5, no. 10 (2021), 1273–81.

Gqokonqana, O., et al. "Blended Learning Challenges During COVID-19: A Case of Cost Accounting 2 Students at a Selected South African Higher Education Institution." *Research in Social Sciences and Technology* 7, no. 2 (2022): 87–107.

Gravett, Karen, and N. E. Winstone. "Making Connections: Authenticity and Alienation within Students' Relationships in Higher Education." *Higher Education Research and Development* 41, no. 2 (2022): 360–74.

Gravett, Karen, et al. "Pedagogies of Mattering: Re-conceptualising Relational Pedagogies in Higher Education." Teaching in Higher Education 29, no. 2 (2024): 388–403.

Gray, J. A., and Melanie DiLoreto. "The Effects of Student Engagement, Student Satisfaction, and Perceived Learning in Online Learning Environments." *International Journal of Educational Leadership Preparation* 11, no. 1 (2016): n.p.

Gray, Rob, and Collison, David. "Can't See the Wood for the Trees, Can't See the Trees for the Numbers? Accounting Education, Sustainability, and the Public Interest." *Critical Perspectives on Accounting* 13, no. 5–6 (2002): 797–836.

Gredley, Susan. Socially Just pedagogies: Toward participatory parity in higher education. PhD diss.: University of the Western Cape, 2022.

Greene, Maxine. "In Search of a Critical Pedagogy." Harvard Educational Review 56, no. 4 (1986): 427–42.

Greenhow, C., et al. "Diverse Perspectives on Improving Contemporary Online Learning Theory, Research and Practice." In *Society for Information Technology and Teacher Education International Conference*,1842–46. Vienna: Association for the Advancement of Computing in Education (AACE), 2023.

Grimes, C. M. "Enhancing Adult Online Learners' Graduate Leadership Experiences Through the Lens of Care Theory." In *Best Practices and Strategies for Online Instructors: Insights from Higher Education Online Faculty*, 167–194. Hershey, PA: IGI Global Scientific Publishing, 2025.

Groccia, J. E. "What Is Student Engagement?" *New Directions for Teaching and Learning* 2018, no. 154 (2018): 11–20.

Gruenewald, D. A. "The Best of Both Worlds: A Critical Pedagogy of Place." *Educational Researcher* 32, no. 4 (2003): 3–12.

Gunn, Simon. "Translating Bourdieu: Cultural Capital and the English Middle Class in Historical Perspective." *The British Journal of Sociology* 56, no. 1 (2005): 49–64.

Gutmann, Amy, and Dennis F. Thompson. *Why Deliberative Democracy?* Princeton, NJ: Princeton University Press, 2004.

Habermas, Jürgen. "Political Communication in Media Society: Does Democracy Still Enjoy an Epistemic Dimension? The Impact of Normative

Bibliography

Theory on Empirical Research." *Communication Theory* 16, no. 4 (2006): 411–26.

Hailikari Terre. "The Relevance of Prior Knowledge in Learning and Instructional Design." *American Journal of Pharmaceutical Education* 72, no. 5 (2008): 113.

Haleem, Abid, et al. "Understanding the role of digital technologies in education: A review." *Sustainable Operations and Computers* 3 (2022): 275–85.

Haley, D. "Unconventional educational approaches: an eco-pedagogy to address our transformative challenges." *Quality Education* (2020): 917–29.

Halpern, David. *Social Capital*. Cambridge, UK: Polity Press, 2005.

Hargreaves, Andy. What the COVID-19 pandemic has taught us about teachers and teaching. *Facets* 6, no. 1 (2021): 1835–63.

Havergal, Chris. "Why Lecturers Must Take Responsibility for Student Success." *Times Higher Education*, 2019.

Hazelton, James, and Haigh, Matthew. "Incorporating Sustainability into Accounting Curricula: Lessons Learnt from an Action Research Study." *Accounting Education: An International Journal* 19, no. 1–2 (2010): 159–78.

Heidemann, Ivonete T. S. B, and Marcia C. P. Almeida. "Friere's Dialogic Concept Enables Family Health Program Teams to Incorporate Health Promotion." *Public Health Nursing* 28, no. 2 (2011): 159–67.

Helm, Francesca, et al. "Global Citizenship Online in Higher Education." *Educational Research for Policy and Practice* 23, no. 1 (2024): 1–18.

Hibbert, L., ed. *English as a Language of Learning, Teaching and Inclusivity: Examining South Africa's Higher Education Crisis*. Milton Park, UK: Taylor & Francis, 2023.

Hill, J., et al. "Pedagogic Partnership in Higher Education: Encountering Emotion in Learning and Enhancing Student Wellbeing." *Journal of Geography in Higher Education* 45, no. 2 (2021): 167–85.

Hillier, Jean, and Rooksby, Emma. 2017. *Introduction to First Edition. In Habitus: A Sense of Place*. London: Routledge, 2017.

Hirst, Elizabeth, and Brown, Raymond. "Pedagogy as dialogic relationship: Fostering cosmopolitan teacher identities." In *Researching International Pedagogies* (2008), 179–99.

Hlatshwayo, Mlamuli N., and Kennedy G. Fomunyam. "Theorising the #MustFall Student Movements in Contemporary South African Higher Education: A Social Justice Perspective." *Journal of Student Affairs in Africa* 7, no. 1 (2019): 61–80.

Hoch, Mary L. "Intercultural Dialogues in Medieval Philosophy: Maimonides on Balancing Individual and Societal Responsibilities." *Dialogue and Universalism* 35, no. 1 (2024): 59–88.

Hodges, Charles, et al. "The difference between emergency remote teaching and online learning." Educause Review, Mar. 27, 2020. https://er.educause.edu/articles/2020/3/the-difference-between-emergency-remote-teaching-and-online-learning

Bibliography

Holcombe, E. M., et al., eds. *Shared Leadership in Higher Education: A Framework and Models for Responding to a Changing World*. Milton Park, UK: Taylor & Francis, 2023.

hooks, bell. *Teaching critical thinking: Practical wisdom*. London: Routledge, 2010.

Hossain, Syed F. A., et al. "Investigating the Role of Social Media on Student Engagement and Authentic Learning during Post COVID-19." In *Virtual Technologies and E-Collaboration for the Future of Global Business*, 68–81. Hershey, PA: IGI Global, 2022.

Hove, N., and Phasha, N. T. "Support services for learners with learning disabilities in mainstream classrooms using capability theory." *South African Journal of Childhood Education* 14, no. 1 (2024): 1–10.

Hughes, J. C. "Bringing Caring, Community and Confrontation into the Academy: Embracing Ubuntu and an Ethic of Care." *The Bloomsbury Handbook of Ethics of Care in Transformative Leadership in Higher Education* (2024): 111.

Hussin, W. N. T. W., et al. "Online interaction in social learning environment towards critical thinking skill: A framework." *Journal of Technology and Science Education* 9, no. 1 (2019): 4–12.

Händel, M., et al. "The webcam and student engagement in synchronous online learning: visually or verbally?" *Education and Information Technologies* 27, no. 7 (2022): 10405–28.

Isaacs, A. "Analysing Educational Leadership in Relation to Deliberative Democracy: Towards a Defensible Form of School Leadership." PhD diss.., University of Stellenbosch, 2021.

Ivancheva, M., and Garvey, B. "Putting the university to work: The subsumption of academic labour in UK's shift to digital higher education." *New Technology, Work and Employment* 37, no. 3 (2022): 381–97.

Ivinson, Gabrielle. "Re-imagining Bernstein's Restricted Codes." *European Educational Research Journal* 17, no. 4 (2018): 539–54.

Jansen, Jonathan D. "Image-ing Teachers: Policy Images and Teacher Identity in South African Classrooms." *South African Journal of Education*, 21, no. 4 (2005): 243–45.

———. "Online Turns Off Connections Crucial to Learning, Teaching." *TimesLIVE*, August 6, 2020. https://select.timeslive.co.za/ideas/2020-08-06-online-turns-offconnections-critical-to-learning-teaching/.

Jarvis, J., and Mthiyane, N. 2022. "Using empathetic-reflective-dialogical restorying as a teaching-learning strategy to confront xenophobic attitudes in a context of higher education." *Journal of Education (University of KwaZulu-Natal)* 88: 107–126.

Jean-François, Emmanuel, ed. *Transnational Perspectives on Innovation in Teaching and Learning Technologies*. Leiden: Brill Sense, 2018.

Jeffrey, Bob, and Anna Craft. "Teaching Creatively and Teaching for Creativity: Distinctions and Relationships." *Educational Studies* 30, no. 1 (2004): 77–87.

Bibliography

Johnston, B., et al. *Conceptualizing the Digital University: The Intersection of Policy, Pedagogy, and Practise.* New York: Springer Publishing, 2019.

Johnstone, Frederick A. *Class, Race, and Gold: A Study of Class Relations and Racial Discrimination in South Africa.* Routledge Library Editions, 2022.

Jones, Peter E. "Bernstein's "Codes" and the Linguistics of "Deficit". *Language and Education* 27, no. 2 (2013): 161–79.

Joorst, Jerome P. "Why Should an Ethics of Care Matter in Education?" *Transformation in Higher Education* 6 (2021): 127.

Joosten, Tanya. *Social Media for Educators: Strategies and Best Practices.* Hoboken, NJ: Jossey Bass Wiley, 2012.

Jung, J., et al. "Exploring teachers' digital literacy experiences." *International Review of Research in Open and Distributed Learning* 25, no. 2 (2024), 41–59.

Kagan, C., et al. *Critical Community Psychology: Critical Action and Social Change.* London: Routledge, 2019.

Kahn, P. E. "Theorising student engagement in higher education." *British Educational Research Journal* 40, no. 6 (2014): 1005–18.

Kane, Robert T., and Jolyn E. Dahlvig. "Traditional Faculty Resistance to Online Higher Education." *American Journal of Qualitative Research* 6, no. 2 (2022): 1–16.

Karakose, Turgut. "Emergency Remote Teaching Due to COVID-19 Pandemic and Potential Risks for Socioeconomically Disadvantaged Students in Higher Education." *Educational Process: International Journal* 10, no. 3 (2021): 53–61.

Karam, Faten J. "Re-envisioning the ESOL Classroom through a Virtues-Based Curriculum: Contributions to Critical Dialogic Education." *TESOL Journal* 12, no. 3 (2021): e582.

Katartzi, Eugenia, and Geoff Hayward. "Conceptualising transitions from vocational to higher education: Bringing together Bourdieu and Bernstein." *British Journal of Sociology of Education* 41, no. 3 (2020), 299–314.

Kaushik, V., and Walsh, CA 2019. "Pragmatism as a research paradigm and its implications for social work research." *Social Sciences*, 8(9): 255.

Keifer-Boyd, Karen, et al. *Teaching and Assessing Social Justice Art Education: Power, Politics, and Possibilities.* London: Routledge, 2022.

Kezar, A. J., ed. *Rethinking Leadership in a Complex, Multicultural, and Global Environment: New Concepts and Models for Higher Education.* Milton Park, UK: Taylor & Francis, 2023.

Kgari-Masondo, Mosa C., and Privilege Chimbunde. "Progress of an African Student during COVID-19 and Beyond in Higher Education: Re-colonisation of Decolonisation?" *Perspectives in Education* 39, no. 1 (2021): 323–39.

Kooy, Mary. "Building a Teacher–Student Community through Collaborative Teaching and Learning: Engaging the Most Affected and Least Consulted." *Teacher Development* 19, no. 2 (2015): 187–209.

Bibliography

Kreber, Carolin. "Academics' Teacher Identities, Authenticity, and Pedagogy." *Studies in Higher Education* 35, no. 2 (2010): 171–94.

Krikowa, N. and Delmo, K. "Reflexive transformative approach to student-centred learning: Insights from the frontlines of Australian higher education teaching during COVID-19." *Journal of Public Relations Education* (2021).

Kuh, George D. "The Other Curriculum: Out-of-Class Experiences Associated with Student Learning and Personal Development." *The Journal of Higher Education* 66, no. 2 (1995): 123–55.

Kumar, Amit, and Nicholas Epley. "Understanding Undersociality: Intentions, Impressions, and Interactions." *Journal of Consumer Psychology* (2023).

Kumar, Ashwani, and Adrian Downey. "Teaching as Meditative Inquiry: A Dialogical Exploration." *Journal of the Canadian Association for Curriculum Studies* 16, no. 2 (2018): 52–75.

Kızılcık, Hale H., and Aylin S. D. Türüdü. "Humanising Online Teaching Through Care-Centred Pedagogies." *Australasian Journal of Educational Technology* 38, no. 4 (2022): 143–59.

Kızıldağ, Ayse, and Isil Kaçar. "Toward More Inclusive Classroom Practices in the Turkish EFL Contexts: A Case Study on the Integration of Critical and Dialogic Approaches to Field Placement." In *Critical Dialogic TESOL Teacher Education: Preparing Future Advocates and Supporters of Multilingual Learners* (2024): 147.

La Fleur, J., and R. Dlamini. "Towards learner-centric pedagogies: Technology-enhanced teaching and learning in the 21st century classroom. *Journal of Education* 88 (2022): 4–20.

Lakey, G. *Facilitating Group Learning: Strategies for Success with Diverse Learners*. Binghamton, NY: PM Press, 2020.

Lambrechts, Wynand, et al. "Decentralizing Emerging Markets to Prepare for Industry 4.0: Modernising Policies and the Role of Higher Education." In *The Disruptive Fourth Industrial Revolution: Technology, Society, and Beyond*, 111–53. Johannesburg: University of Johannesburg, 2020.

Lamont, Michèle, and Annette Lareau. "Cultural Capital: Allusions, Gaps and Glissandos in Recent Theoretical Developments." *Sociological Theory* 6 (1988): 153–68.

Langegård, Ulrica, et al. "Nursing Students' Experiences of a Pedagogical Transition from Campus Learning to Distance Learning Using Digital Tools." *BMC Nursing* 20 (2021): 1–10.

Lareau, Annette. "Social Class Differences in Family-School Relationships: The Importance of Cultural Capital." *Sociology of Education* 4, no. 1 (1987): 73–85.

Lawrence, K.C. and Maphalala, M.C. 2021. Opportunities for social justice in the curriculum and pedagogical practises in higher education institution spaces in South Africa. *Curriculum Perspectives*, 41(2): 143–151.

Bibliography

Le Grange, Lesley, et al. "Education in a 'Neoliberalised' Online Teaching and Learning Space: Towards an Affirmative Ethics." *Transformation in Higher Education* 7, no. 0 (2022): 1–9.

Le Roux, Sarlina G. "Juggling Access vs Retention and Academic Performance: The Experience of a Lecturer Teaching in an Open, Distance e-Learning Institution." *South African Journal of Higher Education* 38, no. 2 (2024): 176–95.

Lefebvre, Elisabeth E., and Matthew A. M. Thomas. "'I knew I had to leave': A Bourdieusian analysis of why Teach For America teachers quit early." *Teaching and Teacher Education* 142 (2024): 104520.

Lemoine, P. A., et al. "Is online learning the future of global higher education?: The implications from a global pandemic." In *Advancing online course design and pedagogy for the 21st century learning environment*, 28–44). Hershey, PA: IGI Global, 2021.

Liambas, Anastasios, and Ioannis Kaskaris. "Dialogue and Love in the Work of Paulo Freire." *Journal for Critical Education Policy Studies* 10, no. 1 (2012): 185–96.

Lin, Nan. *Social Capital: A Theory of Social Structure and Action*. New York: Cambridge University Press, 2001.

Lombard, Petrus. "Factors that Influence Transition from High School to Higher Education: A Case of the JuniorTukkie Program." *African Journal of Career Development* 2, no. 1 (2020): 1–14.

Longo, Nicholas V. "Deliberative Pedagogy in the Community: Connecting Deliberative Dialogue, Community Engagement and Democratic Education." *Journal of Public Deliberation* 9, no. 2 (2020): 1–18.

Longueira, Roxanne. "Exploring the Functionality of the South African Education Quintile Funding System." PhD diss., University of Pretoria, 2016.

Loots, Sonja. *Mapping UFS Students' Journeys: What Works for Student Success. Centre for Teaching and Learning Report.* Bloemfontein: University of the Free State. 2021.

Lorenzen, Mark. "Social Capital and Localised Learning: Institutional Dynamics." *Urban Studies* 44, no. 4 (2007): 799–817.

Lucas, M., and Vicente, P. N. 2022. "A double-edged sword: Teachers' perceptions of the benefits and challenges of online teaching and learning in higher education." *Education and Information Technologies* (2022): 1–21.

Lyons, J., and Tarc, P. 2022. "How might IB classroom pedagogy 'make a better world?'(Toward) illuminating a promising IBDP teacher praxis." *Globalisation, Societies and Education* (2022), 1–20.

Maguire, Cindy, and Tracey Lenihan. "Fostering Capabilities Toward Social Justice in Art Education." *Journal of Cultural Research in Art Education* 28 (2010): 39–53.

Mahadew, A., and D. Hlalele. "Challenging gender certainties in early childhood care and education: A participatory action learning and action research study." *Educational Research for Social Change* 11, no. 1 (2022): 10–26.

Bibliography

Mahlangu, Vimbi. "Creating Caring Learning Environments in Higher Education." *South African Journal of Higher Education* 34, no. 1 (2020): 1–15.

Maigari, P. P. 2021. "A Critique of Charles Taylor's Theory of Recognition." *SOCIETIES: Journal of Social Sciences and Humanities* 1, no. 2 (2021):187–99.

Maistry, Suriamurthee M. "Accountability and Surveillance: New Mechanisms of Control in Higher Education." *Transformation: Critical Perspectives on Southern Africa* 88, no. 1 (2015): 25–35.

Makina, A. "Students' experiences of demotivating online formative assessment strategies at an open-distance learning university." *Perspectives in Education* 40, no. 2 (2022): 32–51.

Makumbe, D. 2020. "E-learning in times of a pandemic: Exposing the economic disparities between the 'haves' and the 'have-nots'." *Journal of Public Administration* 55, no. 4 (2020): 621–41.

Maluleke, W. "Usage of Blackboard Learn for Teaching and Learning in the Historically Disadvantaged Institution: Challenges and Prospects." *South African Journal of Higher Education* 38, no. 5 (2025): 39–62.

Manase, N. *Exploring Experiences of University Students with Learning Disabilities: Shaping Student Engagement in South Africa.* London: Bloomsbury Publishing, 2025.

Maree, K. *First Steps in Research.* Pretoria: Van Schaik Publishers, 2007.

Maringe, Felix, and Nevensha Sing. "Teaching Large Classes in an Increasingly Internationalising Higher Education Environment: Pedagogical, Quality and Equity Issues." *Higher Education* 67 (2014): 761–82.

Maringe, Felix, and Owen Chiramba. *The 4IR and Teacher Education in South Africa: Contemporary Discourses and Empirical Evidence.* Cape Town: AOSIS, 2022.

Maringe, Felix, et al. *Clash of Ideologies in Post-Colonial Education Systems: Convergences and Divergence.* Cape Town: AOSIS Publishing, 2021.

Martin, F. and D. U. Bolliger. "Engagement matters: Student perceptions of the importance of engagement strategies in the online learning environment." *Online Learning* 22, no 1 (2018): 205–22.

Marx, Karl. *Karl Marx on Society and Social Change: With selections by Friedrich Engels.* Chicago: University of Chicago Press, 1973.

Mashiyi, L. N. "Can Old History Textbooks Be Used to Promote the New Democratic Ideals in the Curriculum 2005?" PhD diss., University of the Witwatersrand, 2000.

Matthews, K. E., and M. Dollinger. "Student voice in higher education: The importance of distinguishing student representation and student partnership." *Higher Education* 85, no. 3 (2023), 555–70.

Matthieu, J., and N. Junius. "Educationally Tracked Democratic Equalizers: How Citizenship Education Moderates the Effect of a Political Home Environment on Internal Political Efficacy Across Educational Tracks." *Political Behavior* (2024), 1–23.

Bibliography

Maurissen, Lies, et al. "Deliberation in Citizenship Education: How the School Context Contributes to the Development of an Open Classroom Climate." *Social Psychology of Education* 21, no. 4 (2018): 951–72.

Mawonde, A., and Togo, M. (2021). Challenges of involving students in campus SDGs-related practices in an ODeL context: the case of the University of South Africa (Unisa). *International Journal of Sustainability in Higher Education* 22(7), 1487–1502.

Mayo, P. *Gramsci, Freire and Adult Education: Possibilities for Transformative Action.* London and New York: Zed Books, 1999.

McCabe, A., and O'Connor, U. (2014). "Student-centred learning: the role and responsibility of the lecturer." *Teaching in Higher Education* 19, no. 4 (2014): 350–359.

McCaleb, Sudia P. *Building Communities of Learners: A Collaboration among Teachers, Students, Families, and Community.* London: Routledge, 2013.

McLean, Monica, et al. "A Bernsteinian View of Learning and Teaching Undergraduate Sociology-Based Social Science." *Enhancing Learning in the Social Sciences* 5, no. 2 (2013): 32–44.

McNay, Lois. "The Trouble with Recognition: Subjectivity, Suffering, and Agency." *Sociological Theory* 26, no. 3 (2008): 271–96.

McNeil, Sara, et al. "Facilitating Interaction, Communication, and Collaboration in Online Courses." *Computers and Geosciences* 26, no. 6 (2000): 699–708.

Mehta, Rohit, and Earl Aguilera. "A Critical Approach to Humanizing Pedagogies in Online Teaching and Learning." *The International Journal of Information and Learning Technology* 37, no. 3 (2020): 109–20.

Meletiou-Mavrotheris, M., Eteokleous, N. and Stylianou-Georgiou, A., 2022. Emergency remote learning in higher education in Cyprus during COVID-19 lockdown: A zoom-out view of challenges and opportunities for quality online learning. *Education Sciences* 12(7): 477.

Melvin, W. Y. C., et al. Exploring Controversial Issues in the Primary Social Studies Classroom. *Humanities and Social Science Education* 9, no. 1 (2020): 1–14.

Mhlanga, David. "The Fourth Industrial Revolution and COVID-19 Pandemic in South Africa: The Opportunities and Challenges of Introducing Blended Learning in Education." *Journal of African Education* 2, no. 2 (2021): 15.

Mhlanga, David, et al. "COVID-19 and the Key Digital Transformation Lessons for Higher Education Institutions in South Africa." *Education Sciences* 12, no. 7 (2022): 464.

Mhonda, T. D. J. "South Africa's Post-Apartheid Economic and Education Reforms: A Reversal Of Racial Capitalism?" Master's diss., Eastern Mediterranean University (EMU)-Doğu Akdeniz Üniversitesi (DAÜ), 2020.

Miller, K. E., 2021. "A Light in Students' Lives: K-12 Teachers' Experiences (Re) Building Caring Relationships During Remote Learning." *Online Learning* 25, no. 1 (2021): 115–34.

Bibliography

Miller, P. K. "Hegemonic whiteness: Expanding and operationalising the conceptual framework." *Sociology Compass* 16, no. 4 (2022): e12973.

Mncube, Lancelord S. "Domestication of Open Educational Resources by Academics in an Open Distance e-Learning Institution of South Africa." PhD diss., University of Cape Town, 2022.

Modise, Mphoentle P. "Towards an Effective and Empathetic Student Support System in an Open and Distance Education and E-Learning Environment: A Case Study from a Developing Country Context." PhD diss., University of South Africa, 2016.

Moore, Michael G. *Handbook of Distance Education.* London: Routledge, 2013.

Moore, Rob. *Basil Bernstein: The Thinker and the Field.* London: Routledge. 2013.

Morrow, Wally. *Learning to Teach in South Africa.* Cape Town: HSRC Press, 2009.

Motadi, Richard M. "The Influence of Teachers' Social Class Background on Pedagogic Practice in Gauteng Schools." Master's diss., University of Johannesburg, 2020.

Motala, S., and K. Menon. "In search of the 'new normal': Reflections on teaching and learning during Covid-19 in a South African university." *Southern African Review of Education with Education with Production* 26, no. 1 (2020), 80–99.

Motta, S. C., and A. Bennett. "Pedagogies of care, care-full epistemological practice and 'other' caring subjectivities in enabling education." *Teaching in Higher Education* 23, no. 5 (2018), 631–46.

Mpungose, C. B., and S. B. Khoza, S. B. "Postgraduate student experiences on the use of Moodle and Canvas learning management system." *Technology, Knowledge, and Learning* 27, no. 1 (2022): 1–16.

Mseleku, Z. "Beyond hard barriers: lack of aspiration as a soft barrier to access higher education amongst youth living in low-income housing estate." *South African Journal of Higher Education* 36, no. 6 (2022), 252–69.

Mthabela, Sibongile M. "Exploring the role of Technical Vocational Education and Training College Management in Utilising Learning Management Systems." Master's diss., University of the Free State, 2024.

Mtombeni, Butholezwe. "The Use of Technology in an Open Distance Learning (ODL) Ecosystem to Achieve Authentic Learning." Master's diss., University of Johannesburg, 2020.

Mtombeni, Butholezwe, et al. "Education as a pedagogy of the oppressed: South African education as envisaged by John Langalibalele Dube." *Cogent Education* 12, no. 1 (2025), 2468561.

Mudehwe, F. R. "Dialogic pedagogical innovation for liberating learning practices: A case of one program in a Higher Education Institution in South Africa." PhD diss., University of Fort Hare, 2014.

Munna, A. S., and M. A. Kalam. "Teaching and learning process to enhance teaching effectiveness: a literature review." *International Journal of Humanities and Innovation* 4, no. 2, 1–4.

Bibliography

Munoz, K. E., et al. "Enhancing online learning environments using social presence: evidence from hospitality online courses during COVID-19." *Journal of Teaching in Travel and Tourism* 21, no. 4 (2021): 339–57.

Nagda, B. R. A., et al. "Transformative pedagogy for democracy and social justice." *Race, Ethnicity and Education* 6, no. 2 (2003), 165–91.

Nahal, Sunddip P. "Voices from the Field: Perspectives of First-Year Teachers on the Disconnect Between Teacher Preparation Programs and the Realities of the Classroom." *Research in Higher Education Journal* 8 (2010): 1.

Naidoo, J. "Postgraduate mathematics education students' experiences of using digital platforms for learning within the COVID-19 pandemic era." *Pythagoras* 41, no. 1 (2020): 568.

Nakkula, M. J., and E. Toshalis. *Understanding Youth: Adolescent Development for Educators.* Cambridge, MA: Harvard Education Press, 2020.

Nasim, Kanwal, et al. "Twenty Years of Research on Total Quality Management in Higher Education: A Systematic Literature Review." *Higher Education Quarterly* 74, no. 1 (2020): 75–97.

Navarro, Z. "In search of a cultural interpretation of power: The contribution of Pierre Bourdieu." *IDS Bulletin* 36, no. 7 (2006): 31–46.

Ndlovu, Sifiso. "The pedagogic domain and epistemic access in South African higher education: The challenges for students with disabilities during the COVID-19 pandemic." *South African Journal of Higher Education* 36, no. 4 (2022), 205–24.

Ndofirepi, E. S. "Rethinking Social Spaces in Higher Education: Exploring Undergraduate Student Experience in a Selected South African University." PhD diss., University of the Witwatersrand, 2015.

Neuwirth, L. S., et al. "Reimagining higher education during and post-COVID-19: Challenges and opportunities." *Journal of Adult and Continuing Education* 27, no. 2 (2021): 141–156.

Nguyen, David J. "Low-income students thriving in postsecondary educational environments." *Journal of Diversity in Higher Education* 16, no. 4 (2023), 497.

Ngwenya, Celiwe M. Disruption of Higher Education Policy Through an Ethics of Care in South Africa. PhD diss., Stellenbosch University, 2020.

Ngwoke, H. C., and A. K. Ugwu. "Promoting Innovation for Development through a Participatory-Based Pedagogy: The Freirean Model Considered." *Nnadiebube Journal of Education in Africa* 7, no. 1 (2022).

Niati, Masoud. "Integration of Bourdieu's Habitus into Bernstein's Code." *Open Science Journal* 3, no. 1 (2018): 1–14.

Nicol, C., et al. "Interweaving pedagogies of care and inquiry: Tensions, dilemmas and possibilities." *Studying Teacher Education* 6, no. 3 (2010), 235–44.

Nishiyama, Kei, et al. *Facilitation of deliberation in the classroom: The interplay of facilitative technique and design to increase inclusiveness.* Canberra: University of Canberra, 2020.

Bibliography

Noddings, Nel. "Care Ethics and Education." In *The Handbook of Moral and Character Education*, 92–107. London: Routledge, 2013.

———. *Caring: A Feminine Approach to Ethics and Moral Education*. Oakland: University of California Press, 1984.

———. "The Caring Relation in Teaching." *Oxford Review of Education* 38, no. 6 (2012): 771–81.

———. "Educational Leaders as Caring Teachers." *School Leadership and Management* 26, no. 4 (2006): 339–45.

Northcote, M. "The same but different: Reframing contemporary online education in higher education towards quality and integrity." In *Ensuring quality and integrity in online learning programs*, 1–32. Hershey, PA: IGI Global, 2019.

Nowell, L. S., et al. "Thematic Analysis: Striving to Meet the Trustworthiness Criteria." *International Journal of Qualitative Methods* no. 16, 1 (2017), 1609406917733847.

Nsamba, A. "Maturity levels of student support e-services within an open distance e-learning university." *International Review of Research in Open and Distributed Learning* 20, no. 4 (2019), 60–78.

Obiukwu, N. E. "Influence of Socioeconomic Background on ESL Text Processing of First-year Students in the University in Enugu State." PhD diss., Enugu State University of Technology, 2019.

Oke, A. and F. A. P. Fernandes. "Innovations in teaching and learning: Exploring the perceptions of the education sector on the fourth industrial revolution (4IR)." *Journal of Open Innovation: Technology, Market and Complexity* 6, no. 2 (2020): 31.

Olawumi, K. B., et al. "Situating Ubuntu Philosophy in Pre-service Teacher Education." *International Journal of Learning, Teaching and Educational Research* 23, no. 8 (2024), 605–623.

Olivier, Jako, et al. *Contextualised Open Educational Practices: Towards Student Agency and Self-Directed Learning*. Cape Town: AOSIS, 2022.

Omodan B. I, et al. "Analysis of Human Relations Theory of Management: A Quest to Re-enact People's Management Towards Peace in University System." *South African Journal of Human Resource Management* 18, no. 0 (2020): 1–10.

Onah, I., and A. K. Ugwu. "Kant's Thought Formation and the Role of the Mind: A Groundwork for Development." *Conatus - Journal of Philosophy* 9, no. 1 (2024), 131–155.

Osler, Audrey. "Teacher Interpretations of Citizenship Education: National Identity, Cosmopolitan Ideals, and Political Realities." *Journal of Curriculum Studies* 43, no. 1 (2011): 1–24.

Ovetz, R. "The algorithmic university: On-line education, learning management systems, and the struggle over academic labor." *Critical Sociology* 47, no. 7–8 (2021): 1065–84.

Pacansky-Brock, et al. "Humanizing online teaching to equitize higher education." *Current Issues in Education* 21, no. 2 (2020), 1–21.

Bibliography

Pantazidis, S. "Educating through commons-based pedagogical practices." *EIKI Journal of Effective Teaching Methods* 2, no. 2 (2024).

Papademetriou, C., et al. "COVID-19 pandemic: the impact of the social media technology on higher education." Education Sciences, 12, 4 (2022): 261.

Parker, C., and K. Bickmore, K. "Classroom peace circles: Teachers' professional learning and implementation of restorative dialogue." *Teaching and Teacher Education* 95 (2020): 103129.

Payne, A. L., et al. "Conceptualising and building trust to enhance the engagement and achievement of under-served students." *The Journal of Continuing Higher Education* (2022), 1–18.

Peercy, M. M., et al. 2022. "From humanizing principles to humanizing practices: Exploring core practises as a bridge to enacting humanizing pedagogy with multilingual students." *Teaching and Learning Education* 113, no. 1 (2022): 1036–53.

Pegrum, Mark, and Grace Oakley. 2017. "The changing landscape of e-portfolios: Reflections on 5 years of implementing e-portfolios in pre-service teacher education." In *E-portfolios in Higher Education: A Multidisciplinary Approach*, 21–34. Singapore: Springer, 2017.

Pendergast, Donna, et al. "Engaging Marginalized 'At-Risk' Middle-Level Students: A Focus on the Importance of a Sense of Belonging at School." *Education Sciences* 8, no. 3 (2018): 138.

Peters, R. S. *Ethics and Education.* London: George Allen and Unwin. 1966.

Peterson, Amelia, et al. "Understanding Innovative Pedagogies: Key Themes to Analyze New Approaches to Teaching and Learning." *OECD Working Paper*, no. 172 (2018).

Phejane, M. V. "'The New Normal': A Case Study on the Emergent Transition towards Online Teaching and Learning in Internal Medicine and Anesthesiology at the University of the Free State." *Perspectives in Education* 40, no 1 (2022): 164–78.

Picciano, A. G., et al., eds. *Blended Learning: Research Perspectives, Volume 3.* New York: Routledge, 2021.

Pietersen, Doniwen. "Dialogical, Online Teaching and Learning Platforms in Higher Education: Socially Just and Decolonised." *International Journal of Multidisciplinary Perspectives in Higher Education* 8, no. 1 (2023): 133–47.

———. "Engaging Paulo Freire on Deliberative Democracy: Dialogical Pedagogy, Deliberation and Inclusion in a Transformative Higher Education Online Education Space." *Transformation in Higher Education* 7 (2022): 211.

Pietersen, Doniwen, and Bernadictus Plaatjies. "Freirean Utopian Didactic: A Retrospective View of Education in the South African Education Environment." *Journal of Culture and Values in Education* 6, no. 2 (2023): 123–37.

Pietersen, Doniwen, and Mbusiseni C. Dube. "Black African Postgraduate Students' Authorial Voice in Scholarship." *Research in Social Sciences and Technology* 9, no. 2 (2024): 318–27.

Pietersen, Doniwen, et al. "Techno-Rationalism and Higher Educational Law: Examining Legal Frameworks in Southern African Universities from a Freirean Critical Pedagogy Perspective." *Journal of Culture and Values in Education* 6, no. 3 (2023): 163–78.

———. "Social Capital, Culture, and Codes in Higher Education: Bourdieusian and Bernsteinian Philosophical Underpinnings in the South Africa Environment." *Journal of Culture and Values in Education* 7, no. 2 (2024): 157–72.

Pillay, I. 2021. "Culture, Politics and Being More Equal than Others in COVID-19: Some Psychological Anthropology Perspectives." *South African Journal of Psychology* 51(2): 325–35.

Pitsoe, V. J., and M. M. Letseka. "Social Capital and Open Distance e-Learning: A Bourdieusian and Marxian Discourse." *e-BANGI* 11, no. 1 (2016): 202–12.

Plueger, Cynthia T. "The Lived Experiences of Educators Leveraging Educational Technology and Connectivism for Fostering Academic Achievement in Higher Education: A Transcendental Phenomenological Study." PhD diss., Liberty University, 2024.

Polit, D. and C. T. Beck, C.T. *Essentials of Nursing Research. Appraising Evidence for Nursing Practice.* Philadelphia, PA: Lippincott Williams & Wilkins, 2014.

Pope, Raechele L., et al. *Multicultural Competence in Student Affairs: Advancing Social Justice and Inclusion.* Hoboken, NY: John Wiley and Sons, 2019.

Pouwels, Jan. "We are in need of each other. Paulo Freire and the role of conflicts in education." *International Journal of Social Pedagogy* 7, no. 1 (2019). https://doi.org/10.14324/111.444.ijsp.2019.v7.1.009

Pownall, I. and D. Lock, D., 2022. "Academic Identity during COVID-19." *The International Journal of Pedagogy and Curriculum* 30, no. 1 (2022): 1–15.

Pretorius, Rudi W., et al. "Creating a Context for Campus Sustainability Through Teaching and Learning: The Case of Open, Distance and E-Learning." *International Journal of Sustainability in Higher Education* 20, no. 3 (2019): 530–47.

Price, Deborah, et al. "Richness of Complexity within Diversity: Educational Engagement and Achievement of Diverse Learners through Culturally Responsive Pedagogies." *The Social Educator* 38, no. 1 (2020): 42–53.

Purkarthofer, Eva, and Raine Mäntysalo. "Enhancing Knowledge, Skills, and Identity Development through Collaborative Student-Led Learning: Experiences with the Gradual Empowerment of Students in a Planning Studio Course." *Journal of Planning Education and Research* 44, no. 3 (2024): 1148–159.

Ramirez, G. M., et al. "All-Learning: The State of the Art of the Models and the Methodologies Educational with ICT." *Telematics and Informatics* 35, no. 4 (2018): 944–53.

Reed, Colby D. "Critical pedagogy and the Ethics of Care: How values affect the classroom dynamic." Master's diss., Missouri State University, 2018.

Bibliography

Regan, Annie, et al. Experimental effects of social behavior on well-being. *Trends in Cognitive Sciences* 26, no. 11 (2022): 987–98.

Rhoads, R. A., et al. "The Open Courseware Movement in Higher Education: Unmasking Power and Raising Questions About the Movement's Democratic Potential." *Educational Theory* 63, no. 1 (2013): 87–110.

Ribeiro, L., et al. "First-year students background and academic achievement: The mediating role of student engagement." *Frontiers in Psychology* 10 (2019): 2669.

Richards, K., and B. M. W. Thompson. "Challenges and instructor strategies for transitioning to online learning during and after the COVID-19 pandemic: a review of literature." *Frontiers in Communication* 8 (2023): 1260421.

Richardson, Brooke, and Rachel Langford. "Care-Full Pedagogy: Conceptualizing Feminist Care Ethics as an Overarching Critical Framework to Interrupt the Dominance of Developmentalism Within Post-Secondary Early Childhood Education Programs." *Contemporary Issues in Early Childhood* 23, no. 4 (2022): 408–20.

Richardson, J. W., et al. 2021. "Systematic review of 15 years of research on digital citenship: 2004–2019." *Learning, Media and Technology* 46, no. 4 (2021): 498–514.

Robinson, C. (2012). "Student engagement: What does this mean in practice in the context of higher education institutions?" *Journal of Applied Research in Higher Education*, 4, no. 2 (2012), 94–108.

Robinson, H., et al. "Designing with care: Towards a care-centered model for online learning design." *The International Journal of Information and Learning Technology* 37, no. 3 (2020): 99–108.

RogoÅ, S., and B. BaranoviÄ. "Social capital and educational achievements: Coleman vs. Bourdieu." *Center for Educational Policy Studies Journal* 6, no. 2 (2016), 81–100.

Rossi, V. *Inclusive learning design in higher education: A practical guide to creating equitable learning experiences.* Milton Park, UK: Taylor & Francis, 2023.

Rothwell, Daniela. "Initial Teacher Education Seminars and Minority Ethnic Students: Exploring Dialogic Teaching and Engagement." *Teaching in Higher Education* 30, no. 2 (2025): 444–62.

Rowley, C., et al. "Adopting a student-led pedagogic approach within higher education: the reflections of an early career academic." *Reflective Practice* 19, no. 1 (2018): 35–45.

Ruben, B. D., et al. *A guide for leaders in higher education: Concepts, competencies, and tools.* Milton Park, UK: Taylor & Francis, 2023.

Ruga, L. R. "An Assessment on Reason and Religion in Jürgen Habermas' Philosophy." PhD diss., University of Santo Tomas, Manila, 2014.

Sadovnik A. R. "Basil Bernstein's Theory of Pedagogic Practice: A Structuralist Approach." *Sociology of Education* 1, no. 1 (1991): 48–63.

Bibliography

————. *School, Social Class and Youth. the Way Class Works: Readings on School, Family and the Economy.* London: Routledge, 2008.

Sadovnik, A. R., et al. *Exploring Education: An Introduction to the Foundation of Education.* Boston, MA: Allyn and Bacon, 2000.

Sahlberg, Pasi. "Rethinking Accountability in a Knowledge Society." *Journal of Educational Change* 11, no. 1 (2010): 45–61.

Saidi, A. "Enhancing academic success through the involvement of students in quality assurance and promotion in higher education: A synopsis." *South African Journal of Higher Education* 34, 5 (2020), 1–19.

Sakkoulis, Dimitris P., et al. "In-service training as a factor in the formation of the teachers' individual theory of education." *International Education Studies* 11, no. 3 (2018): 48–60.

Salimi, G., et al. "Impact of online social capital on academic performance: exploring the mediating role of online knowledge sharing." *Education and Information Technologies* 27, no. 5 (2022), 6599–620.

SALUM Report. "National Report: Staff Experiences of, and Perceptions of Teaching and Learning and its Future 2021." *Journal of International and Comparative Education* 10, no. 1 (2020): 33–50.

Samuelsson, M., and S. Bøyum. "Education for deliberative democracy: Mapping the field." *Utbildning and Demokrati–tidskrift för Didaktik och Utbildningspolitk* 24, no. 1 (2015), 75–94.

Sanger, Catherine S. "Inclusive Pedagogy and Universal Design Approaches for Diverse Learning Environments." In *Diversity and Inclusion in Global Higher Education: Lessons from Across Asia*, 31–71. Singapore: Palgrave Macmillan, 2020. https://doi.org/10.1007/978-981-15-1628-3_2

Sarwar, B., et al. "Usage of social media tools for collaborative learning: The effect on learning success with the moderating role of cyberbullying." *Journal of Educational Computing Research* 57, no. 1 (2019): 246–79.

Sathorar, H. and D. Geduld. "Reflecting on Lecturer Dispositions to Decolonise Teacher Education." *Journal of Education (University of KwaZulu-Natal)* 76, no. 1 (2019): 108–27.

Sato, Simone N., et al. "Navigating the New Normal: Adapting Online and Distance Learning in the Post-Pandemic Era." *Education Sciences* 14, no. 1 (2023): 19.

Scanlon, Dylan and Cornelia Connolly. "Teacher agency and learner agency in teaching and learning a new school subject, Leaving Certificate Computer Science, in Ireland: Considerations for teacher education." *Computers and Education* 174 (2021): 104291.

Sedrakyan, G., et al. "Feedback digitalization preferences in online and hybrid classroom: Experiences from lockdown and implications for post-pandemic education." *Journal of Research in Innovative Teaching and Learning* 18, no. 1 (2025), 56–75.

Sekome, N. P., and N. J. Mokoele. "Adapting to eLearning during covid-19: neglecting student diversity in south African higher education." *International Journal of Entrepreneurship* 26, no. 1 (2022): 1–9.

Bibliography

Selco, Jodye I. and Mariam Habbak, M. STEM students' perceptions on emergency online learning during the COVID-19 pandemic: Challenges and successes. *Education Sciences* 11, no. 12 (2021): 799.

Selwyn, Neil. *Is technology good for education?* Cambridge, UK: Polity Press, 2019.

Sequeira, L., and C. M. Dacey. "The COVID-19 diaries: Identity, teaching and learning at the crossroads." *Frontiers in Education* 5, no. 1 (2020): 586123.

Sershan, Naidoo, et al. "Adapting to the New Frontier: The Transformative Role of Academics in Shaping Higher Education." *Acitya: Journal of Teaching and Education* 7, no. 1 (2025): 164–78.

Sevnarayan, K. "Reimaging eLearning technologies to support students: On reducing transactional distance at an open and distance eLearning institution." *E-Learning and Digital Media* 19, no. 4 (2022), 421–39.

Shaffer, Timothy J., and Nicholas V. Longo, eds. *Creating Space for Democracy: A Primer on Dialogue and Deliberation in Higher Education.* Milton Park, UK: Taylor & Francis, 2023.

Shange, Thembeka. "Foregrounding Care in Online Student Engagement in a South African E-Learning University." *Open Praxis* 15, no. 4 (2023): 288–302.

Shanyanana, Rachel N., and Yusef Waghid. "Towards a Re-Imagined Notion of University Education: In Defence of a Reconstituted Ethics of Care." *South African Journal of Higher Education* 28, no. 4 (2014): 1376–97.

Shemshack, Atikah, and Spector, Jonathan M. "A Systematic Literature Review of Personalized Learning Terms." *Smart Learning Environments* 7, no. 1 (2020): 33.

Sherman, Tyrone. "High School Educator Perspectives of a Professional Learning Community Implementation Initiative in a Minority School." PhD diss., Walden University, 2022.

Shi, Jiayi, and Peter Sercombe. "Poverty and Inequality in Rural Education: Evidence from China." *Education as Change* 24, no. 1 (2020): 1–28.

Simon, E. "The impact of online teaching on higher education faculty's professional identity and the role of technology: The coming of age of the virtual teacher." PhD diss., University of Colorado Boulder, 2012.

Sims, S., and H. Fletcher-Wood. "Identifying the characteristics of effective teacher professional development: A critical review." *School Effectiveness and School Improvement* 32, no. 1 (2021): 47–63.

Sincer, I., et al. "Teaching diversity in citizenship education: Context-related teacher understandings and practices." *Teaching and Teacher Education* 78 (2019): 183–92.

Singh, Mankirat, et al. "Determining the Students' Preferable Learning Mode for Both Traditional Classrooms Teaching Under Normal Situations and Forced Virtual Teaching in Quarantine Period." In *2021 IEEE Frontiers in Education Conference (FIE)*, 1–8. Lincoln, NE: IEEE, 2021.

Sinha, A. *Reconfiguring Pedagogy and Curriculum Practice in Light of Online Teaching.* Cham: Springer International Publishing, 2024.

Bibliography

Sinwell, Luke. "Teaching and Learning Paulo Freire: South Africa's Communities of Struggle." *Education as Change* 26, no. 1 (2022): 1–19.

Skakane, Thembekile P., et al. "Exploration of the Procedures and Practices for Providing Student Support Services in a Nursing College in South Africa." *Journal of Student Affairs in Africa* 12, no. 1 (2024): 97–114.

Skerritt, C. "The Code for Success? Using a Bernsteinian Perspective on Sociolinguistics to Accentuate Working-class Students' Underachievement in the Republic of Ireland." *Irish Journal of Sociology* 25, no. 3 (2017): 274–96.

Smith, D. G. *Diversity's promise for higher education: Making it work*. Baltimore, MD: John Hopkins University Press, 2024.

Sousa, A. N. "Dialogue in Online Learning Spaces: How Transitioning to Online Learning during a Pandemic Impacts Classroom Dialogue and Inclusivity." *Journal of Teaching and Learning with Technology* 10 (2021), 229–37.

Spaull, N. Poverty and Privilege: Primary School Inequality in South Africa. *International Journal of Educational Development* 33, no. 5 (2013): 436–47.

Srinivasa, K. G., and G. M. Siddesh. *Confluence of Teaching and Learning Through Digital Pedagogy*. Newcastle upon Tyne, UK: Cambridge Scholars Publishing, 2024.

Stahl, G. *Narratives of Reconstruction in Discourses of Aspiration and Change, Bourdieu, Habitus and Social Research, the Art of Application*. London: Palgrave Macmillan, 2015.

Stephens, N. M., et al. "Social-class disparities in higher education and professional workplaces: The role of cultural mismatch." *Current Directions in Psychological Science* 28, no. 1 (2019): 67–73.

Stone, C. 2022. "From the margins to the mainstream: The online learning rethink and its implications for enhancing student equity." *Australasian Journal of Educational Technology* 38, no. 6 (2022): 139–49.

Stough, Laura M., and Marcia L. Montague. "How Teachers Learn to Be Classroom Managers." In *Handbook of Classroom Management*, 446–458. London: Routledge, 2014.

Streck, D. R. "Pedagogies of Participation: A Methodological Framework for Comparative Studies." In *Global Comparative Education: Journal of the WCCES*, edited by T. N'Dri Assié-Lumumba, 35–49. Cornell University, NY: WCCES, 2017.

Stronach, R. A. "How Does Learning Happen? Ontario's Pedagogy of Oppression: A Critical Discourse Analysis of Ontario's Early Years Pedagogical Framework." *Journal of Childhood Studies* 48, no. 2 (2023): 32–50.

Stubbs, M. "Sociolinguistics of the English Writing System or Why children Aren't Adults." *Australian Journal of Reading* 5, no. 1 (1982): 30–6.

Sullivan, A. "Bourdieu and Education: How Useful is Bourdieu's Theory for Researchers?" *Netherlands Journal of Social Sciences* 38, no. 2 (2002): 144–66.

Bibliography

Sulé, V. Thandi., et al. "The Case for Case Studies: Dialogic Engagement and Case Study Creation in a Higher Education Classroom." *Active Learning in Higher Education* 24, no. 3 (2023): 321–36.

Susen, Simon. "Jürgen Habermas: Between Democratic Deliberation and Deliberative Democracy." In *The Routledge Handbook of Language and Politics*, 43–66. London: Routledge, 2018.

Szreter, S. "The state of social capital: Bringing back in power, politics, and history." *Theory and Society* 31, no. 5 (2002), 573–621.

Tackie, H.N., "(Dis) Connected: Establishing Social Presence and Intimacy in Teacher–Student Relationships During Emergency Remote Learning." *AERA Open* 8 (2022): 23328584211069525.

Tang, A. L. "University students' conceptions and experiences of teacher care amidst online learning." *Teaching in Higher Education* 29, no. 2 (2024), 366–87.

Tate, T. and M. Warschauer. "Equity in online learning." *Educational Psychologist* 57, no. 3 (2022): 192–206.

Tavares, Vander. "A Century of Paulo Freire: Problem-solving Education, Conscientização, Dialogue, and TESL from a Freirean Perspective." In *Social Justice, Decoloniality, and Southern Epistemologies within Language Education*, 145–162. London: Routledge, 2023.

Tinto, Vincent. "Classrooms as Communities: Exploring the Educational Character of Student Persistence." *The Journal of Higher Education* 68, no. 6 (1997): 599–623.

Tjabane, Masebala, and Venitha Pillay. "Doing Justice to Social Justice in South African Higher Education." *Perspectives in Education* 29, no. 2 (2011): 10–8.

Toh, Y. Leading sustainable pedagogical reform with technology for student-centred learning: A complexity perspective. *Journal of Educational Change* 17, no. 2 (2016): 145–69.

Tooley, J. "On School Choice and Social Class: A Response to Ball and Gewirtz." *British Journal of Sociology of Education* (1997): 217–30.

Tripon, C., et al. "Nurturing minds and sustainability: an exploration of educational interactions and their impact on student well-being and assessment in a sustainable university." *Sustainability* 15, no. 12 (2023), 9349.

Tronto, J. C. 2010. "Creating caring institutions: Politics, plurality, and purpose." *Ethics and Social Welfare* 4, no. 2 (2010): 158–71.

———. 2016. Protective or democratic care? Some reflections on terrorism and care. In: Proceedings of the SIGNAL, Cifas, Brussels, 23 September.

———. 2017. There is an alternative: Homines curans and the limits of neoliberalism. International Journal of Care and Caring, 1(1): 27–43.

Turnbull, D., et al. "Transitioning to E-learning during the COVID-19 pandemic: How have Higher Education Institutions Responded to the Challenge?" *Education and Information Technologies* 26, no. 5 (2021), 6401–19.

Bibliography

Tzanakis, M. "Social capital in Bourdieu's, Coleman's and Putnam's theory: empirical evidence and emergent measurement issues."*Educate* 13, no. 2 (2013), 2–23.

UNESCO. 2022. *Reimagining Our Futures Together: A New Social Contract for Education.* Paris: UNESCO, 2022.

University of the Free State (UFS). *Who Are Our Students? Biographical Survey Data Report Faculty of Theology.* Bloemfontein: University of the Free State, 2021.

University of the Free State Centre for Teaching and Learning. *Emergency Remote Teaching at the UFS: An Analysis of the #UFSTeachOn Response.* Bloemfontein: University of the Free State Centre for Teaching and Learning, 2020.

Vally, Salim. "Between the Vision of Yesterday and the Reality of Today: Forging a Pedagogy of Possibility." *Education as Change* 24, no. 1 (2020): 1–24.

Van den Berg, Geesje. "Context matters: Student experiences of interaction in open-distance learning." *Turkish Online Journal of Distance Education* 21, no. 4 (2020): 223–36.

Van der Westhuijzen, Anika. "Ways of Seeing, Knowing and Gathering: Taking Art Out of the Classroom: Exploring the Scope for Art Education in the Expanded Field to Benefit the Transformative Process of Higher Education." PhD diss., Stellenbosch University, 2015.

Van Staden, D., and P. Naidoo. "Future-proofing imperatives for remote online teaching, learning and student support in the context of pandemic change and beyond: A case for South African higher education transformation." *South African Journal of Higher Education* 36, no. 3 (2022), 269–81.

Venter, Anneke. "Exploring the downside to student online collaborations." *The Independent Journal of Teaching and Learning* 19, no. 1 (2024), 335–53.

———. "Social Media and Social Capital in Online Learning. *South African Journal of Higher Education* 33, no. 3 (2019): 241–57.

Von Solms, N. "Exploring the Experiences in Mainstream Schools with the Implementation of the Policy on Screening, Identification, Assessment and Support (2014)." PhD diss., University of the Free State, 2020.

Waghid, Yusef. 2014. "Islamic Education and Cosmopolitanism: A Philosophical Interlude." *Studies in Philosophy of Education* 33(3): 329–42.

Waghid, Y. 2021. Teaching and Learning During a Pandemic: Implications for Democratic Citizenship Education. *Citizenship Teaching and Learning* 16(2): 225–28.

Waghid, Yusef. "Knowledge Production and Higher Education Transformation in South Africa: Towards Reflexivity in University Teaching, Research and Community Service." *Higher Education* 43 (2002): 457–88.

Waghid, Yusef, et al. "The Fourth Industrial Revolution Reconsidered: On Advancing Cosmopolitan Education." *South African Journal of Higher Education* 33, no. 6 (2019): 1–9.

Bibliography

———. "Philosophy of Education in a New Key: Cultivating a Living Philosophy of Education to Overcome Coloniality and Violence in African Universities." *Educational Philosophy and Theory* 54, no. 8 (2022): 1099–112.

———. *Towards a Philosophy of Caring in Higher Education*. Cham: Springer International Publishing, 2019.

Waghid, Z., et al. "Assessing Cognitive, Social and Teaching Presences during Emergency Remote Teaching at a South African University." *The International Journal of Information and Learning Technology* 38, no. 5 (2021): 413–32.

Walker, Melanie, et al. *Low-Income Students, Human Development and Higher Education in South Africa: Opportunities, Obstacles and Outcomes*. Cape Town: African Minds, 2022.

Wallace, R. M. "Online Learning in Higher Education: A Review of Research on Interactions Among Teachers and Students." *Education, Communication and Information* 3, no. 2 (2003): 241–80.

Walton, E., and P. Engelbrecht. "Inclusive education in South Africa: Path dependencies and emergences." *International Journal of Inclusive Education* 28, no. 10 (2024), 2138–56.

Warren, M. J. C. "Teaching with Technology: Using Digital Humanities to Engage Student Learning." *Teaching Theology and Religion* 19, no. 3 (2016): 309–19.

Weber, M. *Methodology of Social Sciences*. London: Routledge, 2017.

Weber, Max. "Charisma and Disenchantment." In *The Vocation Lectures: The Scholar's Work*. New York: Review of Books, 1917.

Wegerif, Rupert. *Dialogic: Education for the Internet Age*. London: Routledge, 2013.

Weisberger, M., et al. "How do technological changes in formal education shape the social roles of teachers who are mothers?" *Teaching and Teacher Education* 103 (2021): 103344.

Whalley, Brian, et al. "Towards Flexible Personalized Learning and the Future Educational System in the Fourth Industrial Revolution in the Wake of Covid-19." *Higher Education Pedagogies* 6, no. 1 (2021): 79–99.

White, J. W., and P. R. Lowenthal. "Minority college students and tacit 'codes of power': Developing academic discourses and identities." *The Review of Higher Education* 34, no. 2 (2011): 283–318.

Whiteside, Aimee L., et al., eds. *Social Presence in Online Learning: Multiple Perspectives on Practice and Research*. Milton Park, UK: Taylor & Francis, 2023.

Williams, R., et al. "AI+ ethics curricula for middle school youth: Lessons learnt from three project-based curricula." *International Journal of Artificial Intelligence in Education* (2022), 1–59.

Winthrop, Rebecca. "The Need for Civic Education in 21st-Century Schools." In *Brookings Institution Policy Brief*. Washington, D. C.: Brookings Institution, 2020.

Bibliography

Wood, B. E., et al. "Pedagogies for Active Citizenship: Learning through Affective and Cognitive Domains for Deeper Democratic Engagement." *Teaching and Teacher Education* 75, no. 1 (2018): 259-67.

Yan, D. and Q. Fan. "Online informal learning community for interpreter training amid COVID-19: A pilot evaluation." *PLoS One* 17, no. 11 (2022): e0277228.

Yee, A. "The Unwritten Rules of Engagement: Social Class Differences in Undergraduates' Academic Strategies." *The Journal of Higher Education* 87, no. 6 (2016): 831-58.

Zawacki-Richter, O., et al. 2019. "Systematic review of research on artificial intelligence applications in higher education – where are the educators? *International Journal of Educational Technology in Higher Education* 16, no. 1 (2019): 1-27.

Zizzamia, Rocco, et al. "Snakes and Ladders and Loaded Dice: Poverty Dynamics and Inequality in South Africa, 2008-2017." *WIDER Working Paper* 2019/25. Helsinki: UNU-WIDER, 2019.

Zongozzi, J. N., and S. A. Ngubane. Equitable access to digital higher education for students with disabilities in South Africa. *African Journal of Disability* 14 (2025), 1525.

Zulu, N. T. "The Struggles and the Triumphs of South African Black Women Professors." *South African Journal of Higher Education* 35, no. 6 (2020): 239-57.

www.ingramcontent.com/pod-product-compliance
Lightning Source LLC
Chambersburg PA
CBHW060355090426
42734CB00011B/2140